COMMON SENSE

A New Approach to Understanding
Scripture

DAVID W. BERCOT

SCROLL
PUBLISHING

If a man learns without preconceived ideas,
he has ears to hear the truth.

Clement of Alexandria

Contents

1

The Mad Philosopher

As the morning sun rose over the cobblestone streets of ancient Athens, a strange figure climbed out of a giant water urn, where he had spent the night. Clothed in a dirty, ragged gown, he tramped through the narrow, crooked streets of the city. As he walked, his white hair and flowing white beard reflected the morning rays of the sun. Although it was broad daylight, he carried a lighted lantern as he doggedly plodded through the streets, jostling his way through the milling crowds.

Making his way to the noisy, crowded marketplace, he approached one man after another, holding his lantern up to their faces, and scrutinizing every line of their countenances. Amid the clatter of horses and the shouts of vendors hawking their wares, onlookers stared curiously at this crazed eccentric.

"What are you doing, you madman?" someone shouted sarcastically from the throngs.

"My name is Diogenes," he replied testily, "and I'm searching for an honest man."

If Diogenes carried his lantern into today's churches, would he find an honest man or woman? The reason I ask is that this is primarily a book about honesty.

By the term "honesty," I'm not referring to restraint from stealing or lying. Rather, I'm speaking of *intellectual* and *spiritual* honesty. That is, the willingness to be totally objective in the pursuit of God's truth. Intellectually honest Christians have the desire and the ability to see all sides of any spiritual or theological issue. They are far more concerned about finding out *what is true* than they are about defending their personal positions or the positions of their denomination or church.

Actually, spiritual and intellectual honesty should come naturally to all Christians. Scripture tells us that God is a God of truth (Ps. 31:5). A person who is truly reborn of God intensely desires to imitate his Father. As Jesus stated, "Those who worship Him must worship in spirit and *truth*" (Jno. 4:24, italics mine).

So if your burning desire is not for truth, I'm afraid you have wasted your money in purchasing this book. If you desire simply to find support for your personal or denominational interpretations of Scripture, then there is no point in reading any further. Your desire will be much better satisfied by reading only the literature published by your church or denomination.

However, if your heart aches for truth, if your fervent yearning is to worship God in spirit and truth, then I only ask that you prayerfully and honestly weigh what I have to say.

But let me say at the outset that this is *not* a book about David Bercot's interpretation of Scripture. I'm not saying that if you are interested in truth then you must follow *my* personal interpretation of Scripture. In fact, the message of this book is just the opposite: I'm saying that what David

Bercot thinks Scripture means is totally irrelevant. I'm in no better position to accurately understand Scripture than you are. If the choice is between your interpretation and mine, you might as well keep your own interpretation.

Why This Book Is Needed

So what am I saying? I'm saying quite frankly that the approaches to Scripture that we Bible-believing Christians have taken do not work. Not one of them has provided a realistic means for all Bible-believing Christians to become one body again.

Despite all the systems of Biblical interpretation that have been promoted since the Reformation, each century has found the body of Christ further and further fragmented. Today, professing Christians are divided into over *22,000* different denominations and sects, with an average of five new ones organized every week.[1] And, generally speaking, none of these denominations and sects are answerable to any of the other groups. Furthermore, nearly all of these denominations have been established since the Reformation.

If you think that Christ doesn't object to His body being fragmented into thousands of schisms, think again. The primary thing on His mind before He was arrested was the unity of the Church. He prayed, "Neither pray I for these alone, but for them also which shall believe on me through their word; That they all may be one; as thou, Father, art in me, and I in thee, that they also may be one in us" (Jno. 17:20,21 KJV).

Yet, we Protestants think nothing of tearing off another chunk of flesh from Christ's body. We don't recognize factionalism for being the perilous sin that it is. Paul lists it as one of the "deeds of the flesh ... of which I forewarn you just as I have forewarned you that those who practice such things shall not inherit the kingdom of God" (Gal. 5:19,21). He told Titus, "Reject a divisive man after the first and second admonition, knowing that such a person is warped and sinning, being self-condemned" (Tit. 3:10,11 NKJV). Perhaps that Scripture condemns all of us Bible-believing Christians today. We are "divisive" men and women. We are "warped and sinning." And we and our predecessors have made a mess out of the body of Christ.

Throughout this book, I will be using the term "Protestant" rather loosely to include all professing Christians who do not belong to either the Roman Catholic Church or to one of the Orthodox eastern churches. In other words, when I use the term, I'm including mainline Protestants, evangelicals, charismatics, Anabaptists, and other non-catholics. I realize that many of these groups don't consider themselves to be Protestants. I don't particularly consider myself to be one either. But this book will read a lot more smoothly if you will allow me to use the term "Protestant" in such a loose, collective sense, rather than individually naming all of the non-catholic groups each time I address them.

And to one degree or another, nearly all of us "Protestants" have done our part to splinter the body of Christ even further. Not only are we not repentant over our sectarian spirit, we even want to make God an accomplice in our sin. How often I have heard evangelical Christians say, "It's important to go to the church where God wants *you.*" In other words, God wants John Doe to go to one certain church, Mary Jones to go to another, and Bob Smith to go to still another. We delude ourselves into thinking that Christ *wants* a divided body—despite His specific prayer to the contrary.

Despite its shortcomings, the Roman Catholic Church has at least been able to remain a single body. In contrast, from the very beginning the Reformers were divided against each other. The passage of time has only made those divisions worse. Even false religions have a better track record than do Bible-believing Christians. Islam is far older than the churches that have come out of the Reformation. Yet, it is divided into relatively few groups. And even those groups will normally worship together at the same mosque when in a foreign country.

No, it's not normal for a religious group to fragment into 22,000 thousand sects in a period of less than 500 years. It is something bizarre. And, when Christians do it, it is something quite sinful.

"But what can I do about it?" you may ask. "It's not my fault that there are so many denominations and divisions." And in a sense that is true. Most of us are not the ones who started the various denominations and sects. Yet, most of us share the same mentality and spirit of those founders. And if we aren't working toward a solution, then *we* are part of the problem.

Make no mistake about it. There *is* a solution to the problem of division. Bible-believing Christians who truly love God can all be one. And I'm not talking about ecumenical unity based on compromising foundational Christian truths and commandments.

Rather, the message of this book is that, to a large degree, our divisions are a result of our illogical approaches to Scripture. So the solution is a new approach to Scripture. By "new" I am not referring to some strange or esoteric system of Bible interpretation. I'm speaking of just the opposite. This "new" approach is so obvious and elementary that it's simply—common sense.

2

A Tale of Two Lawyers

The defense attorney had been brilliant. Witness after witness had wilted before his withering cross-examination. He had fought the crucial procedural battles like a military tactician. And his closing argument to the jury was delivered with such feeling that several members of the jury were in tears. The jury deliberated only a brief time before rendering their verdict: "Not guilty!"

Yes, the brilliant attorney had won. But Truth had lost. For the accused man had actually committed the crime. His lawyer had won by suppressing crucial evidence (legally, of course). But to the lawyer, truth was quite irrelevant. The point of the trial was not truth. Rather, the point was to obtain a "Not Guilty" verdict from the jury.

A trial attorney's methodology is to start out with a biased mind. A mind that has already decided that his or her client is in the right. A trial attorney's task is not to determine the truth. Rather, it is to line up as much evidence as possible to support his client's case. And, if legally possible, to suppress and leave hidden all evidence that would hurt his client's case.

The sad fact is that trial lawyers and theologians are twin brothers. Incredibly few theologians start out with a blank slate and a mind open to God's truth. Rather, like trial lawyers, they begin with a preconceived idea—that their school of theology is correct. They look at Scripture as a pool of verses from which to gather statements that support their theology. And they ignore or explain away verses that don't.

As Victorian author, Samuel Butler, observed, "A clergyman, again, can hardly ever allow himself to look facts fairly in the face. It is his profession to support one side; it is impossible, therefore, for him to make an unbiased examination of the other."[1]

And just as trial lawyers try to legally suppress all evidence that doesn't support their case, many theologians have likewise tried to suppress viewpoints and relevant evidence that doesn't support their theology. In fact, compared to theologians, lawyers seem rather civilized in their treatment of their opponents. In times past, theologians generally silenced an opponent by having him burned at the stake, or by torturing him until he recanted his views.

It wasn't just the Roman Catholics who tortured and killed those who opposed their theology. Lutherans, Calvinists, Anglicans, and Puritans did the same thing as well. Since torture and execution are no longer viable options, today's theologians often try to bury their opponents in a barrage of epithets and denunciations. In doing so, Protestant theologians are simply following the example of the founder of the Reformation: Martin Luther. In his book, *The Bondage of The Will*, which was written in answer to Erasmus' book on free will, Luther addressed Erasmus with earthy language and contempt:

So that it seems even superfluous to reply to these your arguments, which have been indeed often refuted by me; but trodden down, and trampled under foot, by the incontrovertible Book of Philip Melanchthon "Concerning Theological Questions": a book, in my judgment, worthy not only of being immortalized, but of being included in the ecclesiastical canon: in comparison of which, your Book is, in my estimation, so mean and vile, that I greatly feel for you for having defiled your most beautiful and ingenious language with such vile trash.[2]

In court, no lawyer would be allowed to address his opponent in such contemptible language. But all is fair in theological wars. Luther's methodology reminds me of an anecdote I heard a speaker share at a conference:

The church custodian was cleaning out the church building one Monday morning. As he was dusting off the pulpit, he noticed that the minister had left his sermon notes on the pulpit. So the custodian began to curiously leaf through the notes. He soon noticed that the minister had written various speaking cues in the margin of his notes. Alongside one paragraph, the minister had scrawled: "story about mother and baby—speak softly and tenderly." Alongside another paragraph, he had scribbled: "motivational point—speak confidently and enthusiastically." There were many more such notes written in the margins. However, the note that particularly caught the custodian's attention was one that said: *"weak point—yell like mad!"*

Unfortunately, there is a bit of truth to the story. Theologians are often the most dogmatic on matters where their Scriptural support is the weakest. And where their ground is the shakiest, they are often the quickest to label their opponents as heretics.

A Different Kind of Law

When I compare theologians to trial lawyers, I do not do so out of conjecture. For I *am* a practicing attorney myself. And I am also an earnest student of Scripture. I have witnessed firsthand how both trial lawyers and theologians function.

However, I no longer practice trial law, as I found too many conflicts between it and the teachings of Christ. So I now limit my practice almost exclusively to title examination. And title examination requires an entirely different type of thinking than does trial work. In Texas (where I practice law), as in most states, obtaining a deed to a tract of land does not assure a buyer that he is actually receiving clear *title* to that land. In order for a buyer to be certain that he or she is obtaining clear title, he or she must either purchase title insurance or have an attorney examine the chain of title to the land.

My primary client is Texas Utilities Mining Company, a subsidiary of an electric company that purchases land containing deposits of coal and lignite. Before purchasing such land, my client wants to be assured that it is obtaining good title both to the land and to the coal and lignite. My job is to read and analyze every single document that affects title to the land. My client pays me to be absolutely objective, unbiased, and even nit-picky.

In the world of trial law, what the jury *thinks* the truth to be is infinitely more important than the actual truth. However, in the world of title law, the actual truth is what matters. The fact the seller thinks he has good title is fairly irrelevant. I am paid to find out the truth about the title to the land—even if it contradicts what others think. And sometimes what I uncover pleases nobody. Yet, my client would have it no other way. The last thing my client wants is to mine the coal and lignite, and *then* find out that someone else owns title to it.

If we humans see the need for objective honesty when land titles are at stake, how much more should we see this need when *eternity* is at stake? Yet, ironically, when eternity is at stake, we pursue truth by using the methods of a trial lawyer. We begin with our minds already made up, and then we build a case from proof-texts to support the verdict that we have already come to.

But if we truly want to please God, we can't approach Scripture in this manner. Instead, we must approach Scripture with the same unbiased, objective honesty that a title lawyer employs in his work. If we don't, we never will find the truth.

Now I'm going to make a rather bold claim. I would not make such a claim unless I truly believed it with all my heart. The claim is this: If we Bible-believing Christians would simply use the same common sense principles of interpretation that title lawyers use, we could all be one body again.

We're going to take a look at those principles. But before we do, there are a few things we need to understand about truth.

3

Rules of Truth

When I examine title to a tract of land, I realize the conclusions that I come to will in no way affect how title to the property *is actually owned.* In other words, my conclusions cannot alter the truth. If I were to convince my client erroneously that its title were clear, I would only succeed in hurting my client. The title itself would not be affected.

This is the first thing we need to understand about truth:

> *What we believe to be true*
> *does not in anyway change*
> *what is actually true.*

In other words, the truths about God, his Son, our salvation, punishments and rewards after death, baptism, and a host of other spiritual subjects are not affected in the least by what you and I believe. If I could persuade every single person in the world to accept all of my beliefs, it would not make those beliefs correct. Nor would it change what is actually true.

I think we all would claim to recognize this principle. In fact, probably *nobody* would claim that he thinks he can change eternal truths by what he believes. But our actions show otherwise. The fact is we *do* purposefully ignore Scriptures that oppose our doctrines. We *do* refuse to admit that other interpretations of key Scriptures might be correct. Scholars *do* slant their translations of Scripture to fit their own preconceptions. And we *do* choose translations that fit our biases, or those of our pastors. In fact, most of us refuse to even look at evidence that might prove that our interpretations are wrong.

Yes, in our sub-conscious minds, we really do think we can change eternal truths by manipulating Scripture or hiding evidence. What utter fools we are! As Winston Churchill said, "Truth is incontrovertible. Panic may resent it; ignorance may deride it; malice may distort it; but there it is."[1]

Until a person truly believes in the uttermost depths of his soul that he cannot alter truth, he will never properly understand Scripture. And until he believes without question that he has nothing to fear from truth, he will not even *want* to make an honest search for truth.

"But how do I know whether or not I truly believe this principle—that truth is unchangeable?" you might ask. The answer is: You believe it when you are able to read Scripture with the same objectivity and detachment with which a title lawyer reads a deed. That is—when you can approach Scripture with no other desire than to know what Scripture *really* means. But there is a barrier that prevents most of us from doing that. That barrier is called *preconceived beliefs*.

Preconceived Beliefs

Several years ago, during a visit to Harlingen, Texas, my wife and I were browsing through a carpet store, looking over all the richly-colored samples of carpet. In addition to selling carpet, the store was also an authorized dealer of Electrolux vacuum cleaners. My wife and I were standing a few feet from the counter when a woman came up to the owner and asked her, "What brand of vacuum cleaner do you recommend?" What do you think the owner said?

Naturally, the owner said she recommended Electrolux vacuum cleaners. But she was not a disinterested party, was she? She already had preconceived ideas about the subject.

That's our main problem when we read Scripture. We already have preconceived ideas of what we will find before we even turn the pages.

> *Preconceived beliefs are a barrier to finding truth.*

As one ancient writer put it, "It is impossible to teach someone something he thinks he already knows." If we are convinced that we already know what the correct teachings of Scripture are, then we can read Scripture over and over and yet never see anything different from what we already believe. To be open to receive truth, we must start with a blank slate.

But most of us are never given that opportunity.

How We Arrive at Our Belief Systems

Although I now limit my practice to title work, I used to handle a limited number of lawsuits. And aside from court-appointed cases, I have never lost a lawsuit. Brilliant attorney? Hardly! I'm barely competent in a courtroom. I won nearly all of my cases simply because the other side never showed up. In law, we call this a default judgment. The worst lawyer in the world can win a default judgment.

Unfortunately, most Christians have acquired their doctrinal beliefs through "default judgment." It is not very difficult to convince another person that a given set of theological doctrines are "the truth" when equal time is not allowed for an opposing set of doctrines.

Let's take the case of Peter Hawkins. He was raised in a godly home. Both of his parents were committed members of an Assembly of God church. They inculcated Pentecostal beliefs in Peter from the time he was a young boy. By the time Peter was an adult, he thoroughly knew all of the fundamental holiness doctrines, and he could defend them quite adroitly from Scripture. He would laugh at the suggestion that he acquired his beliefs by default judgment. "No, I believe what I do because that is what the *Bible* teaches," he would tell you quite confidently.

Mary Rodriguez has a testimony that is a bit different. She was raised in a Roman Catholic home. Her mother went to Mass fairly regularly; her father went less frequently. Her parents rarely prayed at mealtimes (or at any other time), and they almost never read their Catholic Bible. By the time Mary graduated from high school, she had quit attending Mass altogether. She soon was regularly using illegal drugs and living immorally.

One day a fellow worker named Janet told Mary how she could have a personal relationship with the Lord. She showed Mary several verses from Scripture that demonstrated the need for Mary to recognize herself as a sinner, to repent of her sins, and to accept Jesus as her Savior. Mary earnestly prayed to Jesus and invited Jesus into her heart. She thereafter began to regularly attend a local Baptist church with Janet. She enrolled in a "New Members" Sunday school class, where she learned what the Bible teaches on various subjects. Today, she is still a faithful member of the same Baptist church. Like Peter, she would adamantly deny that she acquired her beliefs by default judgment. No, she believes what she does "because that's what the Bible teaches."

Despite their denials, Peter and Mary are classic examples of Christians who have acquired their beliefs by default judgment. As a child or as a new believer, only one version of the gospel was ever presented to them. Ever since, they have read Scripture through the theological eyes of the church to which they belong.

Both Peter and Mary are now quite aware that there are numerous other versions of the Gospel out there. And they even know what Scriptures others "twist" in order to support their doctrines. Peter can clearly show anyone why Mary's version of the gospel is in error, and Mary can likewise show anyone why Peter's version of the gospel is in error.

Unless you belong to one of the "unreached people groups" that has never heard the gospel—unless you have never had any contact with other Christians—then you too have preconceived ideas about what Scripture says. That does not mean your preconceived ideas are incorrect. Nor does it mean that there is something wrong with the fact that you have preconceived ideas. Parents *should* instruct their children in what they believe to be true. Churches *should* provide Biblical instruction to their members.

So preconceived ideas are normal. But that does not change the fact that they are a barrier to finding truth.

When Was the Last Time
You *Listened* to Scripture?

Because of our preconceived beliefs, most Christians have never truly experienced what it is like to actually *listen* to what the Bible writers are saying. Instead, when we read Scripture, all of the preconceived ideas that were inculcated in us as children or as new Christians drown out the actual words of the Bible. We see the words on the pages of our Bibles. And we *think* we are hearing those words. But in reality, we are often hearing only the words of our teachers, not the words of the Bible.

Let me illustrate what I mean. I was raised to believe that all humans inherit the guilt of Adam's original sin. Maybe that's correct theology; maybe it's not. The correctness of that theology is not at issue here. As a child, I was shown Romans 5:12 as proof of this teaching: "Through one man sin entered into the world, and death through sin, and so death spread to all men, because all sinned."

As a result, every time I used to read Romans 5:12, my mind was hearing the verse say: "Through one man sin entered into the world, and death through sin, and so death spread to all men because all men inherited the sin and guilt of Adam." My mind always heard the words of my teachers, not the actual words of Scripture. And so I was absolutely convinced that *Scripture* taught that we inherit both the sin and the guilt of Adam. If anyone denied that principle, I considered them to be ignoring the plain language of Scripture.

It took me nearly 30 years to ever realize that I was hearing preconceived interpretations, not the plain language of Scripture. To be sure, the theory that we inherit the guilt of Adam's sin is a plausible explanation of Romans 5:12. Perhaps it is the correct explanation. But there are other plausible interpretations of that verse. And none of us will ever be able to actually listen to Scripture until we learn to separate our doctrinal beliefs—our "plausible explanations"—from the actual language of Scripture.

In summary, two of the basic rules of truth are: (1) what we believe to be true does not change what is *actually* true, and (2) preconceived beliefs are a barrier to finding truth. Now that we recognize those two characteristics of truth, we're ready to look at some of the common sense principles of interpretation that we title lawyers use.

The Blank Slate

When my clients give me a title abstract to examine, they want me to begin with a blank mental slate. In other words, they don't want me to have any preconceived ideas as to what sort of title problems I'm going to uncover when I examine that abstract. The *last* thing my clients want me to do is to examine title with a slanted mindset. They don't want me to "build a good case" that the person from whom they are planning to purchase the land has clear title. A biased, slanted title examination would be worthless to them.

That exemplifies the first common sense principle of interpretation:

Principle No. 1

*To find truth, you must
start with a blank slate.*

"So where does that leave us?" you might ask. "Since we all have preconceived ideas, how can we ever discover the truth?" Don't be alarmed. There is a way. In fact, the battle is half won once a person recognizes and admits that his slate is *not* blank. In other words, we can't have a blank slate until we first admit that we *don't* have one.

I realize that it's hard for most of us to admit we have preconceived beliefs. I was thirty-seven years old before my eyes were rudely awakened. I then came to see how many preconceptions I actually had. Before then, I would have vehemently denied that I had *any*.

How do you know when you are reading Scripture with a blank slate? The answer is: When you have no theological system to defend. When you have no prior conclusions to which Scripture must be molded. Admittedly, that is a very difficult state to obtain. But I'll show you an initial short-cut to get you started.

Let's suppose that you were going to do a study of what the Scriptures teach about salvation. You would be an unusual Christian, indeed, if you don't presently have any beliefs on that subject. So we're not going to pretend that those preconceptions are not there. Rather, we will try to work around them.

As you look at Scriptures pertaining to the subject of salvation, ask yourself: "If I were raised in a pagan society and had never read the Bible before, what would this verse seem to be saying to me?" In other words, "*If I didn't know any better,* what would I probably think this verse was saying?"

That's the first step. Now, let's look at some of the other common sense principles of interpretation.

4

Principles of Interpretation

When I pulled the package out of my mailbox, I knew exactly what was inside of it. It was more abstracts from Texas Utilities Mining Company. (An abstract is a compilation of all of the deeds and other instruments affecting the chain of title to a particular tract of land.) I was in store for another day or two of dull reading. Yet, hundreds of thousands of dollars would hinge on my interpretations of the reams of deeds and other documents contained in the abstracts. With that much at stake, I couldn't afford to just guess about things. No, I had to use reliable principles of interpretation.

The first principle of interpretation we have considered is basically common sense: Begin with a blank slate. The second principle is just as basic: Start at the very beginning.

I always begin a title examination by first reading the Patent. The Patent is the instrument by which the government originally conveyed the land to a private owner. In Texas, this usually means going back to sometime before 1850—often back to when Mexico owned the land. Once I have studied the Patent, I then trace the title forward,

20

reading every single deed, lease, will, mortgage, lien, and other instrument that may affect title to the land. I would never dream of skipping over to the twentieth century, when deeds began to be typewritten, and beginning at that point.

Likewise, when interpreting any single document, such as a deed or a will, I always start at the beginning. I don't skip down to the middle of the document and then start reading.

This same principle applies to Scripture. When searching for the truths of Christianity, this means going back to the words of Jesus himself. This is a rather obvious principle, yet here the majority of evangelical Christians get side-tracked. They begin with Paul, not Jesus. Many evangelicals virtually ignore Jesus' teachings—claiming that they apply to an earlier dispensation, or to the "kingdom age." Others re-shape Jesus' words in order to make them fit Paul's words.

How very strange. Jesus said, "A disciple is not above his teacher" (Matt. 10:24). Yet, we make Paul, the disciple, greater than Jesus, the Teacher. We subordinate Jesus to Paul; we understand Jesus' words only in the context of Paul's writings. In sharp contrast, the early Christians understood Paul in the context of Jesus' teachings. Their gospel was, above all, the gospel of Jesus.

Principle No. 2

Start at the beginning: with the teachings of Jesus.

Our upside-down approach to Scripture is a fairly new tradition. It began with Martin Luther, who said that the Book of Romans is "the chief part of the New Testament."[1]

We may not use his exact words, but in practice we follow in his footsteps.

However, a common sense approach to Scripture requires us to begin with the Author of Christianity, Jesus Christ—not with Paul. In our illustration of discovering what Scripture teaches about salvation, it means that we begin with the four Gospels.

The American Law Institute states another common sense principle that document lawyers use: "Where language has a generally prevailing meaning, it is interpreted in accordance with that meaning."[2] In other words, begin by giving all words their ordinary, plain meaning.

Principle No. 3

When reading Scripture, begin by giving each sentence its literal meaning if taken alone.

In applying this principle to our illustrative study of salvation, it would mean that as you read through the New Testament, give each verse its plain, literal meaning. At this stage, don't worry about trying to harmonize any verse with what other verses may have to say. That will come later.

At the same time, it's essential that you look at every statement in the New Testament that pertains to salvation—or that *may* pertain to salvation. No sentence in Scripture was intended to stand alone. Statements in one portion of the Bible often intermesh with statements made elsewhere. That's true for all written documents.

For that reason, the American Law Institute has laid down this additional principle: "A writing is interpreted as a whole, and all writings that are part of the same transaction are interpreted together."[3] Restating this in the context of Scripture interpretation, we have:

Principle No. 4

Look at every statement in Scripture that applies, or could apply, to the topic being considered.

In short, it is not enough to simply give each passage in Scripture its most natural, literal meaning. It is equally important to consider all of the passages of Scripture that relate, or that might relate, to the subject under consideration.

Putting It All Together

Now let's review these four common sense principles we have considered up through this point:

1. Begin with a blank slate.
2. Start at the beginning: with the teachings of Jesus.
3. When reading Scripture, give each sentence its literal meaning if taken alone.
4. Look at *every* statement in Scripture that applies, or could apply, to the topic being considered.

After finishing this book, I encourage you to follow these steps to see what the Scriptures *really* teach about salvation. I did that very thing several years ago. But I'm not going to

tell you what conclusions I came to. I want to see what
conclusions you come to on your own. Besides, I don't want
to digress by getting into a protracted discussion about a
major theological issue.

Rather, for the sake of brevity, let's begin with a topic
about which the New Testament has very little to say: the
woman's prayer covering. In fact, only one passage in the
New Testament even discusses this subject: 1 Corinthians
11:1-16. The prayer covering makes an ideal topic for our
discussion because nobody would regard it as one of the key
doctrines of Christianity. So we should be able to talk openly
and honestly about it without getting sidetracked from our
real topic: *understanding Scripture.*

This subject is ideal in another way: it will really put our
system to the test. That's because 1 Corinthians 11:1-16
contains several ambiguous statements that modern Christians have interpreted in a variety of ways. Let's read this
passage together, keeping in mind our four principles of
interpretation:

> Be imitators of me, just as I also am of Christ.
> Now I praise you because you remember me in
> everything, and hold firmly to the traditions, just as
> I delivered them to you. But I want you to under-
> stand that Christ is the head of every man, and the
> man is the head of a woman, and God is the head of
> Christ.
>
> Every man who has *something* on his head while
> praying or prophesying, disgraces his head. But
> every woman who has her head uncovered while
> praying or prophesying, disgraces her head; for she
> is one and the same with her whose head is shaved.
> For if a woman does not cover her head, let her also
> have her hair cut off; but if it is disgraceful for a

woman to have her hair cut off or her head shaved, let her cover her head.

For a man ought not to have his head covered, since he is the image and glory of God; but the woman is the glory of man. For man does not originate from woman, but woman from man; for indeed man was not created for the woman's sake, but woman for the man's sake. Therefore the woman ought to have *a symbol of* authority on her head, because of the angels.

However, in the Lord, neither is woman independent of man, nor is man independent of woman. For as the woman originates from the man, so also the man *has his birth* through the woman; and all things originate from God. Judge for yourselves: is it proper for a woman to pray to God *with head* uncovered?

Does not even nature itself teach you that if a man has long hair, it is a dishonor to him, but if a woman has long hair, it is a glory to her? For her hair is given to her for a covering.

But if one is inclined to be contentious, we have no other practice, nor have the churches of God.*

Now let's discuss this passage in light of our common sense principles, and see if we can all come to the same understanding. In light of our discussion of truth, let's remember from the outset that regardless of how we interpret this passage it will not in any way change what God is

---

*This quotation is taken from the New American Standard translation. However, any other fairly literal translation will work just as well for our study. The reader should note that italics are used in the New American Standard to indicate that the words italicized do not appear in the Greek text, although they may be implied by the Greek. They are not used to denote emphasis.

saying here. What *we* believe will in no way alter what *God* requires.

Our first principle of interpretation is to begin with a blank slate. But we can't do that until we first acknowledge what preconceived understandings we may have. Depending on what church you belong to, you may have any one of the following preconceived ideas about this text:

- Paul is saying that men must not wear any veil or cloth covering on their heads when praying or prophesying, but women must wear a cloth veil or other cloth covering when praying or prophesying.

- Paul is saying that women must not cut their hair, for their long hair serves as a covering when they are praying or prophesying.

- Paul is directing the sisters to veil themselves so as to not be mistaken as prostitutes, since the prostitutes in Corinth did not veil themselves. Being a cultural thing, these instructions do not apply today.

- Paul is directing each sister to wear her hair long so as to not be mistaken as a pagan priestess, since it was customary for a pagan priestess to shave herself bald or to cut her hair short. Once again, these instructions do not apply today.

Or, you may have some other preconceived understanding of this passage. But whatever your understandings of this passage are, I'm now going to ask you to *temporarily* set them aside. I'm not making this request because what you believe about this passage is necessarily wrong. I don't even know what you believe about it. But I do know that there are widely conflicting interpretations of this passage — and that they can't all be right.

Now, having temporarily set aside all of your views, the next step is to read through this passage again very slowly, verse by verse. Start at the beginning,* and as you read each verse, ask yourself, "*If I didn't know any better*, what would I probably think that this verse was saying?"

It's very important that at this stage you do not attempt to harmonize any single verse with any other verses — either in this passage or elsewhere. That will come later. At this point, the important thing is to really *listen* to what each individual verse or statement of Scripture is saying. We're after the literal meaning of each verse—if that verse stood alone. The whole is the sum of the parts, and we can't arrive at the whole picture if we ignore any of the parts.

If there were another portion of the New Testament that discussed this same matter, we would next want to go to it and repeat this same procedure. However, this is the only place in the New Testament that discusses the head covering. So the final step is to now put the literal meanings of all of these individual verses together. I encourage you to take a moment to do this.

Does the System Work?

What conclusions have you ended up with? My guess is: the same thing you started with. Why? Because the four principles we have considered are not sufficient by themselves to tackle a difficult passage such as this. This passage contains several ambiguous statements. That is, those statements can be interpreted in more than one way. When

---

*In this case we aren't starting with the four Gospels because none of the Gospels address this subject.

it comes time to harmonize our literal readings of each verse, we simply run back to our preconceptions. After all, our minds are not like blackboards. Most of us cannot simply erase something from our minds once it's been embedded there. Quite often, our preconceived views don't move until something else shoves them aside.

Let's focus for a moment on some of the ambiguities in this passage. Verse 5 clearly states that a woman disgraces her head if she prays with her head uncovered. Yet, verse 15 states that "her hair is given to her for a covering." Does this mean that her hair serves as the covering referred to in verse 5? Some people say it does; others say it does not.

Other parts of this passage are equally unclear. What did Paul mean when he said in verse 16: "But if one is inclined to be contentious, we have no other practice, nor have the churches of God"? Was Paul saying that the churches of God had no custom other than for the women to cover their heads? Or was he saying that they had no custom either way?

Our four principles are inadequate because they don't tell us how to resolve conflicts and ambiguities such as we have here. But it was important to go through this procedure so that you would appreciate the need for some additional principles of interpretation.

Actually, the lack of clarity in this passage makes it ideal for our study. It forces us to deal squarely with one of the reasons why Bible-believing Christians are so disunited: *Many passages in Scripture—perhaps most—can be interpreted in more than one way.* I'm not saying that all the diverse interpretations are correct or even plausible. I'm simply saying that humans always find a variety of ways to interpret a large number of Biblical passages. Yet, only one of those interpretations is normally correct.

That Scripture is often ambiguous may seem like a fairly obvious, common sense observation (which it is!). But failure to recognize this fact is one of the main reasons we Bible-believing Christians have such a theological log jam. Our refusal to admit that much of Scripture is capable of being interpreted in more than one way is one of the biggest obstacles to Christian unity.

And it is only after we acknowledge this that we can begin to make some real progress toward accurately understanding Scripture. Let me explain.

5

Why Human Language Is Unclear

The reason that Bible-believing Protestants and evangelicals are so divided today is not because the Reformation eventually was derailed. No, it's because the Reformation was never on the right track to start with. In fact, an astute observer in the days of Martin Luther could have quite easily predicted the result of the Reformation: the splintering of the body of Christ.

The reason I say this is that, almost to a man, the Reformers failed to recognize (or refused to admit) that most passages in Scripture are capable of being interpreted in more than one way. Instead, the Reformers steadfastly maintained that Scripture is quite clear and unambiguous. Persons who did not interpret Scripture the way any particular Reformer did were simply "enemies of God who refused to accept what Scripture plainly teaches."

For example, Martin Luther brashly declared that Scripture is totally clear. He denounced those who said otherwise with every invective imaginable:

Therefore come forward, you and all the Sophists together, and produce any one mystery which is still abstruse in the Scriptures. But, if many things still remain abstruse to many, this does not arise from obscurity in the Scriptures, but from their own blindness or want of understanding. . . . Let, therefore, wretched men cease to impute, with blasphemous perverseness, the darkness and obscurity of their own heart to the all-clear Scriptures of God. . . .

If you speak of the external clearness, nothing whatever is left obscure or ambiguous; but all things that are in the Scriptures, are by the Word brought forth into the clearest light, and proclaimed to the whole world. . . . In a word, if the Scripture be obscure or ambiguous, what need was there for its being sent down from heaven? . . . .

But I fear I must already be burdensome, even to the insensible, by dwelling so long and spending so much strength upon a point so fully clear; but it was necessary, that the impudent and blasphemous saying, 'the Scriptures are obscure,' should thus be drowned. . . . Therefore they who deny the all-clearness and all-plainness of the Scriptures, leave us nothing else but darkness.[1]

Somehow the Reformers never came to grips with the obvious: If the Scriptures are "all-clear" and "all-plain," then why were the Reformers themselves unable to agree on what Scriptures teach? Why did the Reformation, with its slogan of "Sola Scriptura," create such a patchwork of conflicting denominations and sects?

Sadly to say, the Bible-believing Protestant churches have never recovered from the obstinacy of Martin Luther.* Christians today still impetuously assert that the Scriptures are completely clear and can reasonably be interpreted in only one way. Yet, those very same Christians are quite unable to agree on just what it is that the Scriptures "clearly teach."

That is why I said at the outset that this is a book about honesty. If we cannot be honest about ambiguities in Scripture, we will never be able to find the true meaning of Scripture. And we will never be able to be one body again.

This Is Not an Attack on Scripture

Let me make it quite clear that I strongly believe in the inspiration and inerrancy of Scripture. I believe it to be the only inspired source of written authority for Christians. Recognizing the ambiguity of human language is not an attack on the authority or inspiration of Scripture. It is simply being honest. The problem is not that there is some sort of deficiency in *Scripture*, but that our languages are not a perfect means of communication.

As an attorney, I have experienced firsthand the difficulty of drafting a contract that is not capable of being interpreted in more than one way. Even when I write a contract with the utmost care, I often find that there are still some ambiguous statements in it. And when we attorneys try to draft a contract that covers all contingencies and is free of all ambiguities, we usually end up with something nearly as

---

*We are all indebted to Martin Luther for getting Western Christians back into the Bible in the first place. Without his pioneering work, perhaps the Bible would still be a closed book to most of us. Yet, Luther's obstinacy poisoned the very Reformation that he began.

thick as a telephone book. Usually nobody but another attorney can even understand it! (It's for good reason that God didn't use attorneys to write the Bible.)

Of course, the Holy Spirit's means of communication are infinite. But God chose to communicate His truths through our finite human languages, just as He has chosen imperfect humans to be His co-workers. After Paul had been caught up into Paradise, he said the things he heard were "inexpressible" in human language (2 Cor. 12:4). Perhaps many of God's other truths are inexpressible in our languages.

Why Human Language Is So Inexact

A few months ago, my wife Deborah and I went out to eat at a restaurant with another couple, Rhonda and David. Rhonda and I both ordered chicken for our main course. Rhonda ordered the pineapple chicken, along with a baked potato. I ordered the Santa Fe chicken, along with rice. When our server brought the meals to our table, Rhonda and I looked at the tray in dismay. My Santa Fe chicken came with her baked potato, and her pineapple chicken was sitting quite attractively on my bed of rice.

Our original waiter noticed that there was some problem, and he quickly came over to our table to find out what was wrong. When we told him about the mix-up, he apologized and very politely asked us, "Would you like for me to handle it for you?" Rhonda and I both quickly replied that we would.

Then, as we sat there watching, to our utter astonishment, the waiter grabbed hold of the pineapple chicken with his hands and placed it on Rhonda's plate with her baked potato. He then picked up the Santa Fe chicken with his hands and dropped it on my bed of rice. To say that we were all quite stunned would be an understatement. (This wasn't a truck stop!) As the waiter nonchalantly walked away, Rhonda muttered under her breath, "I wonder where his hands have been today?"

Why did his actions astonish us? It was because Rhonda and I had assumed that when the waiter asked, "Do you want me to *handle* it for you?" he meant, "Do you want me to *take care of* it for you?" (That's the fourth definition of "handle" in my Webster's Dictionary.) However, the waiter was meaning, "Do you want me to *touch it with my hands?*" (That's the first definition of "handle" in Webster's Dictionary.)

As a lawyer, I know all too well how this sort of misunderstanding happens every day. Virtually every word in the English language has more than one meaning. Flip through a collegiate dictionary sometime, and you will see what I mean. In fact, a large percentage of our words have three or more possible meanings. For example, my dictionary gives forty-four different meanings for the word "hand." When words are joined together in a sentence, it usually eliminates most of the possible meanings. Yet, it still often leaves us with more than one possibility.

This situation is not unique to English. Other languages are similar. So it's not the fault of Scripture that many Bible passages can be interpreted in more than one way. It's simply a reflection of our imperfect human languages.

Other Reasons Why Scripture Is Unclear

The ambiguity of human languages would be enough by itself to create ambiguity in Scripture. However, the problem is further complicated by the fact that our Bible is a collection of works written during a span of about 1500 years, by about forty different men. The New Testament alone was written by at least eight different writers over a period of about fifty years. The majority of the New Testament works are letters, often written to a specific person or congregation.

It should come as no surprise, then, that we sometimes find that the literal language of one part of Scripture contradicts the literal language of another portion of Scripture. Perhaps the classic example is the comparison of Ephesians 2:8,9 with James 2:24. Paul wrote to the Ephesians, "For by grace are ye saved through faith; and that not of yourselves: it is the gift of God: Not of works" (KJV). Yet, James wrote, "Ye see then how that by works a man is justified and not by faith alone" (KJV).

I very much believe that the same Holy Spirit inspired both of those verses to be written. And I therefore believe that those verses can be harmonized. But the issue here isn't *how* those verses can be harmonized. The point is that they *need* to be harmonized. Because the literal language of those verses is contradictory, or at least seems to be contradictory.

The presence of such seemingly contradictory passages in Scripture should come as no surprise. In ordinary speaking or writing, we all say contradictory things. Sometimes (unlike Scripture) this is simply due to our imperfection and forgetfulness. But much of the time the contradictions come because we are addressing different issues, at different times. A statement we make on one occasion is not necessarily intended to apply to another occasion or another issue. Let me give you an illustration.

One of the first secretaries I had was a mature woman who liked to second-guess everything I wrote. Sometimes she would come back to me with a letter I had dictated and say something like, "Are you *sure* this is what you want to say? Wouldn't it sound better if you said such and so?" Sometimes her comments were helpful, but oftentimes she merely wasn't familiar with the language we attorneys use when writing to one another. On several occasions, she simply took it upon herself to change things I had written without asking me. So one day, with a bit of irritation in my voice, I told her, "When I dictate a letter to you, please type it just the way I dictated it! Don't change a thing!"

Several years later, I was working with a younger secretary. Her shortcoming was just the opposite. With her, it was "garbage in, garbage out." If there was a glitch in the dictating equipment, and some words of a sentence got left out, she would just go on typing, ignoring the fact that what she was typing didn't make any sense. If I addressed a letter to a Mr. Smith, but then in my absent-mindedness began the letter, "Dear Mr. Jones," she would type it exactly the way it was given. So one day I told her, "Look, when I give you something to type, think about what you're typing. If it doesn't make sense, come and ask me. Don't just type it the way it is."

So here I gave almost opposite instructions to these two secretaries. Was this because I didn't know what I really wanted? No, I knew what I wanted. Neither set of instructions was intended to be a complete set of guidelines by itself. I was addressing different situations at different times. So I said differing things to fit the occasions.

We find similar situations in Scripture. For example, Jesus told the Pharisees, "He who is not with Me is against Me" (Luke 11:23). Yet, later He told His disciples, "He who is not against us is for us" (Mk. 9:40). Did Jesus not know what he meant? Of course He did! He simply was addressing two different groups of people about differing issues. Neither statement was intended to be an absolute truth in all situations.

What Scripture Is Not

Yet, there is still another reason that Bible-believing Christians cannot agree on the meaning of Scripture. It's because so many of the doctrines we fight over are never directly or thoroughly addressed in Scripture in the first place. The New Testament does not contain a nicely summarized list of Christian doctrines. It doesn't even contain a basic statement of faith. None of the New Testament works were intended to be theological treatises on a given subject.

So most of the doctrines that we cull from the Bible are from statements that are made while the Bible writer was in the course of addressing some other subject. A classic example is Colossians 2:11,12: "In Him you were also circumcised with a circumcision made without hands, in the removal of the body of the flesh by the circumcision of Christ; having been buried with Him in baptism, in which you were also raised up with Him through faith in the working of God, who raised Him from the dead."

Many Christians have used this passage to argue for a particular mode of baptism. And that's not necessarily a misuse of this passage. However, Paul's subject was not the mode of baptism. He simply made a brief reference to baptism in the course of discussing our relationship with Christ.

Once we admit that much of Scripture is ambiguous, we can begin looking for an answer to *resolve* those ambiguities. However, I'm not going to give you my answer quite yet. Instead, I want to examine with you some of the popular approaches Christians use to resolve these ambiguities. Unfortunately, none of them work.

6

Systems That Don't Work

Let's begin by looking at three of the most popular methods of interpreting Scripture. Although all three of the systems have some merit, they all three fall quite short of the mark.

"Let the Clear Passages Interpret the Unclear"

It had been a very special evening. About twenty-five people had come over to our house to hear a godly speaker talk about "The Incredible Christian" and to spend some time together in prayer and fellowship. In fact, it was after 11 p.m. by the time everyone had left. Yet, after the rest of the family had gone off to bed, the speaker and I, along with another brother, sat up on into the night talking about various spiritual subjects.

As the hours ticked away (until 3 a.m.), we moved from one topic to another. We eventually ended up talking about the Scriptural view of divorce and remarriage. The issue is a bit thorny because of the seemingly conflicting statements made by Jesus on the subject. As recorded in Luke 16:18, Jesus said, "Everyone who divorces his wife and marries another commits adultery; and he who marries one who is divorced from a husband commits adultery." But, as recorded in Matthew 19:9, Jesus said, "Whoever divorces his wife, *except for immorality,* and marries another woman commits adultery" (italics mine).

The passage from Luke mentions no exceptions to the matter, but the passage from Matthew adds the phrase, "except for immorality" [Gr. *porneia*]. The three of us talked about how to resolve this apparent conflict. One of the brothers mentioned that he had just read a book pertaining to divorce and remarriage. The author had proposed the solution: "Let the clear passage interpret the one that is not clear."

I agreed that this was a fairly valid principle, "But how does it apply to the present case?" I asked.

The brother replied, "The passage from Luke is clear; the one from Matthew is not. So the passage from Luke controls."

"Well, even though I agree with the principle," I replied, "I don't agree with that application of the principle here. It seems to me that, standing alone, each passage is rather clear. The only thing that is unclear is how the passages relate to each other."*

That, unfortunately, is the inherent weakness of this principle: None of us can agree on what is clear and what is unclear. A person's preconceived ideas invariably influence his assessment of what Bible passages are clear and what are not. However, even if we could agree on what is clear and

---

*This is not intended to be a comment on the merits of the divorce issue, but only a comment on the hermeneutical principle involved.

what is unclear, this principle would not always lead us to the truth. Let me illustrate.

We are all familiar with the words of Jesus, "Blessed are the poor in spirit, for theirs is the kingdom of heaven" (Matt. 5:3). Probably most of us would agree that the phrase, "the poor in spirit," is capable of more than one interpretation. I know I've heard at least three different explanations of this phrase. No doubt many more have been proposed. Some say the "poor in spirit" are those who are free from materialism. The "poor in spirit" might be monetarily wealthy, but their use of their wealth makes them poor as to the "man inside." But others say the phrase means "low in spirits" or "downtrodden." Still others say that the phrase means "spiritually impoverished." People who propose this latter interpretation contend that Jesus was really saying, "Blessed are those who *recognize* their spiritual poverty."

But now, let's look at the parallel passage found in Luke: "Blessed *are* you *who are* poor, for yours is the kingdom of God" (Lk. 6:20). In contrast to Matthew, Luke's rendition is quite clear: blessed are the poor. There is no room for misunderstanding here. But does that mean then that Jesus never said the words, "poor in spirit"? Should we just ignore Matthew's version and accept only Luke's because it is more clear? If it's not fair to do that here, is it fair to do it anywhere else?

Furthermore, how can this principle help us to understand the passage we have been discussing from 1 Corinthians 11? What are the clear parts of that passage? Which parts are unclear? I don't think we would come to any kind of consensus. Of course, we would probably never want to use the *unclear* verses of Scripture to interpret those that are clear. Yet, forcing the unclear passages to fit the clear passages may not lead us to truth, either.

"Let the Many Interpret the Few"

Another principle frequently used is letting the majority of the verses control the few. And there is a considerable amount of validity to this method. After all, where there are seeming contradictions in Scripture on a given doctrine, it would hardly make sense to ignore the majority of the verses in favor of the one or two. Yet, I'm not so sure that it is right to ignore the one or two, either. Just because a particular account or teaching in Scripture does not find support in other passages, that does not make it invalid.

To illustrate, let's look at the accounts given in the four Gospels about the slave who had his ear cut off when Jesus was arrested. Matthew gives us this description of the account: "And behold, one of those who were with Jesus reached and drew out his sword, and struck the slave of the high priest, and cut off his ear. Then Jesus said to him, 'Put your sword back into its place; . . . '" (Matt. 26:51,52). Mark's account is nearly identical.

However, John's account differs slightly: "Simon Peter therefore having a sword, drew it, and struck the high priest's slave, and cut off his right ear; and the slave's name was Malchus. Jesus therefore said to Peter, 'Put the sword into the sheath. . . . '" (John 18:10,11). Finally, Luke gives us the following description of this same event: "And a certain one of them struck the slave of the high priest and cut off his right ear. But Jesus answered and said, 'Stop! No more of this.' And He touched his ear and healed him" (Lk. 22:50,51).

All four gospel writers describe this event, and their accounts are generally in agreement. But only Luke states that Jesus restored the slave's ear. Since the other three accounts make no mention of this, do we simply ignore what Luke says about the ear being restored? Again, only John identifies Peter as the swordsman. Since the other three do not say this, do we just ignore John's statement?

Do you see my point? The principle, "Let the many interpret the few," is usually not valid when applied to historical passages of Scripture. So, is it any more valid when applied to doctrinal subjects? Let's see.

Only four or five verses* in the New Testament directly address Jesus by the title "God." But there are dozens of passages that address His humanity. Do we, therefore, accept only the passages that speak of His humanity? Do we ignore or refuse to believe the passages that tell of His Deity? Of course not! Often, the "few passages" in Scripture contain important truths that must not be ignored by forcing them to fit the "many passages."

Once again, would this principle help us to understand the passage from 1 Corinthians 11? Not at all. What are the "few" passages? What are the "many" passages?

"Go to the Root of the Words"

Another very popular method of attempting to clarify or harmonize Scripture is the use of etymology. Etymology is the branch of language studies that traces words back to their origin and development. It is very popular today for writers or speakers, when delineating Scriptures, to discuss the various root meanings of the Greek words used by the New Testament writers.

This often makes for some very interesting and instructive sermons. And it usually sounds quite logical. But is etymology really a valid tool to use in interpreting Scripture? Let's

---

*John 1:1, 1:18, 20:28; Tit. 2:13; and Heb. 1:8. This varies between translations.

see how much sense it makes in interpreting documents written in English:

Joe Bob Richards owned a sprawling ranch in West Texas. He raised cattle on the ranch, which provided him with a moderate income. However, what was *underneath* the ranch was far more valuable than what was on top. About a mile underneath the surface, there lay valuable deposits of oil and natural gas. In fact, the royalties from the oil and gas enabled Joe Bob to eventually retire. So he sold his ranch to an Italian immigrant, Mario Rossini.

In his deed to Mr. Rossini, Joe Bob Richards reserved all of the "oil, gas and other minerals," a typical reservation found in many Texas deeds. Mario recognized that the climate of West Texas was quite similar to that of some of the Mediterranean countries where olives are grown. So he planted a vast olive orchard, and soon began processing and bottling "Rossini's Pure Virgin Olive Oil" from a factory and warehouse built upon the former ranch.

Mario's olive oil venture was an instant success, and he soon became quite prosperous. However, one day the sheriff came by and delivered a citation to Mario, notifying him that he was being sued by Joe Bob Richards for the value of all the olive oil produced from the ranch. Mr. Richards was claiming that the reservation of "oil, gas and other minerals" included olive oil.

In court, Mr. Richards produced an English professor from Texas Tech University in Lubbock as an expert witness. As the professor accurately explained to the jury, our word "oil" comes from the Latin word *oleum,* which was derived from the Greek word, *elaia,* which means "olive." "Therefore," he argued, "the reservation of 'oil, gas and other minerals' would clearly include olive oil." How do you think the jury voted?

Well, they laughed both Joe Bob Richards and his English professor right out of court. When Texans speak of "oil and gas," they are referring to petroleum, not olive oil. The root origin of the word "oil" is quite irrelevant. And that's true of any other word. If you wanted to know what the writers of the Constitution *really* meant, would you hire a linguistics professor to explain the root meanings and derivations of all of the key words in the Constitution? Of course not!

That's simply a matter of common sense. In the English language, we can immediately see how ludicrous it is to try to interpret a document by using etymology. And what is ludicrous in English doesn't suddenly become logical when we switch to Greek. When you and I write letters to someone, are we cognizant of the root meanings of the words we are using? Do we intend the recipients of our letters to look at the root meanings of our words when they read our letters? Of course not! So why should we think it was any different with Paul and his readers?

Let's face it, most people don't even *know* the root origins of the words they use. I certainly don't. Did you know that our word "gas" comes from a Greek word meaning "chaos"? I didn't. I was also surprised to learn that the root word for employee means "to fold," and that the root meaning of "coin" is "wedge." I could go on and on. Generally speaking, a word means whatever the general population understands it to mean. As a result, meanings change over a period of time. So the root word from which a term is derived is generally irrelevant.

In interpreting 1 Corinthians 11, our quest should be to determine what Paul's words meant in *his* day—not what they meant when they were first coined centuries earlier. Paul wasn't writing to Greek grammatical scholars, schooled in etymology. His readers were probably not even aware of the origins of the words he used.

In summary, all three of the principles discussed here have some validity. But not one of them has been able to bring Christians to any consensus on the meaning of Scripture. And none of them is really of much help in deciphering our passage from 1 Corinthians 11. So now let's look at a system that *can* decipher that passage for us.

7

What Would You Do
in Real Life?

Let's pretend for a moment that we are not talking about interpreting *Scripture*. Instead, let's suppose we are talking about interpreting a letter you received from a friend. How would you clear up ambiguous passages in his letter? I know what I would do. I would write him and *ask* him what he meant. Wouldn't you do the same?

Now, the Bible is a real book, written by real people, living in a real world. Paul was a real man, and the Corinthians were real people. What do you think the Corinthians did if some of the things in Paul's letter were not clear to them? What would you or I have done? We would have asked Paul what he meant, wouldn't we?

In the course of my title work, I frequently read deeds and other documents that are ambiguous or self-contradictory. What do you think I do to interpret these instruments? Well, if the parties to the document are still living, I often ask my client to contact the parties to the deed and ask them what they meant. That is simply common sense. A person doesn't need a law degree to know to do that. It's what you would do in the same circumstance.

So if the Corinthians did not understand what Paul meant, they asked Paul to explain it. But, more than likely, they understood exactly what Paul was talking about. Why? Because Paul was communicating to *them,* not to *us.*

For there to be communication between two persons, there must be what we lawyers call "a meeting of the minds." That is, the mind of the speaker and the mind of the hearer must be united. To use modern terminology, their minds must be on the same wavelength; they must be in sync.

When Paul wrote to the Corinthians, there was a meeting of the minds. However, the minds that met were not ours and Paul's. Paul probably had no idea that you and I would be reading his letter nineteen hundred years later.* No, the minds that came together were Paul's and the Corinthians'. Paul was purposefully communicating to the Corinthians. He was not purposefully communicating to you and me.

Scripture Was Not Written in a Vacuum

Paul's letter to the Corinthians was not written in a vacuum. A considerable amount of background information surrounded the letter. First of all, Paul had spent a year and six months in Corinth, founding and shepherding the congregation there (Acts 18:1,11). In 1 Corinthians 11:2, Paul stated, "Now I praise you because you remember me in

---

*The Holy Spirit, of course, knew this. But Paul seems to have thought that the return of Christ was much closer than it actually was.

everything, and hold firmly to the traditions, just as I delivered them to you."*

So the Corinthians had already received numerous oral traditions directly from Paul. Apparently, his teaching on the head covering was one of those traditions. Paul did not have to explain everything to the Corinthians, as he would if he were writing the letter to us. The Corinthians already knew what Paul was talking about.

Not only had the Corinthians heard Paul teach for eighteen months, they had visibly seen Paul live out his Christianity. So Paul could tell them, "Be imitators of me, just as I also am of Christ" (1 Cor. 11:1). When Paul said, "Every man who has *something* on his head while praying or prophesying, disgraces his head" (v. 3), the Corinthians knew what Paul meant because they had literally watched Paul pray. They knew whether Paul was talking about long hair or talking about a cloth covering, for they had seen him.

While Paul was in Corinth, he lived for awhile with two faithful disciples, Aquila and Priscilla. I think we can safely assume that Aquila and Priscilla obediently followed Paul's teaching on the head covering. So, again, the Corinthians were eyewitnesses of Paul's approved practice on this subject, both as to women (Priscilla) and to men (Paul and Aquila).

They were eyewitnesses of many other things. They had literally watched Paul baptize people, and they had seen other baptisms performed with his approval. So they knew beyond any doubt *how* he baptized people. They had personally shared communion with Paul and had eaten love

---

*The King James Version improperly uses the word "ordinances" here, instead of "traditions." No doubt, this was due to Protestant bias against the word "tradition."

feasts with him. So they knew how often and in what manner those ordinances were kept.

Besides those things, after Paul had left Corinth, he had written them a letter that preceded what we call "1 Corinthians" (1 Cor. 5:9-11). In a sense, then, what we call "1 Corinthians" is actually "2 Corinthians." The Corinthians had read a previous letter from Paul that we do not have access to. Some of the matters addressed in our 1 Corinthians are a follow-up to things he had previously written them.

Furthermore, the Corinthians had also previously written a letter to Paul (1 Cor. 7:1). So part of his letter to them is a reply to their previous letter. Finally, Paul had received other reports of some of the things going on in the Corinthian congregation (1 Cor. 1:11; 11:18). So 1 Corinthians wasn't written in a vacuum. There had been a lot of interaction between Paul and the Corinthians. There was a meeting of their minds.

If that wasn't enough, Paul told the Corinthians that he would be returning there to follow up on his letter. "The remaining matters I shall arrange when I come" (1 Cor. 11:34). Did he actually return there? Apparently so, for he seems to have written his letter to the Romans from Corinth.* So, even if something in Paul's letter hadn't been clear to the Corinthians, they would have been able to ask Paul to clarify those things.

I think, then, we can safely say that the Corinthians accurately understood what Paul was saying in his letter. After all, if *they* didn't, then what hope is there for *us*?

---

*Paul's references to Macedonia, Achaia, and Cenchrea, geographical places near Corinth, point to Corinth as the probable place the letter to the Romans was written (Rom. 15:26;16:1).

But What About Us?

"All that may be nice," you might be thinking, "but how does that help us? We haven't heard Paul teach. We haven't visibly seen Paul in action. We haven't carried on any correspondence with Paul. And we aren't able to ask him to clarify his letter."

That's all true. Asking Paul would be the best approach. But since we can't do that, we need to look at the next best approach. What would that be? To consult with the original Corinthians who received Paul's letter. As we have seen, they almost assuredly understood everything Paul was saying. Unfortunately, we can't ask the Corinthians, any more than we can ask Paul. No, but we are getting much closer now. What we *can* do is look at what attorneys call the "course of performance." Let me illustrate.

The Course of Performance

Ezra Mast was a skilled Amish craftsman who handcrafted beautiful chairs. Although his workshop was in Ohio, his reputation for high quality work traveled quite far. James Butler, who owned a quality furniture store in Topeka, Kansas, came across some of Ezra's chairs. Impressed by the workmanship, he contacted Ezra and soon the two entered into a contract. The basic terms of the contract were that Ezra would make ten chairs each month for Butler's Furniture Store, and Mr. Butler would purchase these chairs at a stated price, adjusted periodically for inflation.

For twenty years, Mr. Butler and Mr. Mast carried on this business relationship. The same contract served them this entire time. When Ezra Mast died, his family sold his workshop and business to Bob Thompson. About the same time, James Butler retired, sold his furniture store to Tom Cook, and moved overseas. The new owners became successors to the original Mast-Butler contract.

It was the fifteenth of the month and Tom Cook had not yet received his chairs. Somewhat impatiently, he called up Bob Thompson and asked, "Where are the ten chairs for this month?"

"Well, they're right here," Bob replied. "I was wondering what was taking you so long to come and pick them up."

"Pick them up? You're supposed to deliver them here."

"No, I'm not. You're supposed to pick them up."

What was the problem? It was that the contract did not address the issue of delivery at all.

How do you think the men resolved this deadlock? What would be the common sense thing to do? "Ask Mr. Butler and Mr. Mast what *they* did," you might answer. But Mr. Mast is dead, and Mr. Butler is overseas. "Then ask their family or employees." Exactly. And if family and employees are not available, we should look at other evidence, such as trip logs and the testimony of people in the community.

In law, we refer to this as the "course of performance." The same principle is true in Scripture, and it's our fifth principle of interpretation:

Principle No. 5

When Scripture is ambiguous, look at the course of performance of the disciples of the apostles.

In law, if a portion of a contract is ambiguous, we look at how the parties themselves interpreted that contract. After all, they best know what they meant. And their actions in performing the contract are the best evidence of the meaning they gave to the contract.

Similarly, in reading Scripture, if we can't ask Paul or the Corinthians what 1 Corinthians means, we *can* look at their course of performance. We can find out how the Corinthians interpreted Paul's letter by looking at their performance and practices.

But where do we get the evidence of their course of performance?

8

Good Sources, Bad Sources

To find out what the practices or "course of performance" was of the New Testament churches, your first inclination may be to grab your trusty commentary or Bible encyclopedia. But that's the *wrong* place to go. I learned that—not from seminary—but from law school and law practice.

That might sound strange, but law school and law practice indelibly impressed on me the need to always go to the *primary sources* when searching for truth about *any* subject. "Primary sources" are the original sources from which other material is derived. To go to the primary sources is to go straight to the horse's mouth.

To illustrate, the primary sources for the teachings of John Wesley are the actual writings and sermons of John Wesley. If you want to be absolutely certain about what John Wesley taught, you must go to his actual writings and sermons. Now, if someone were to read those writings and sermons, and then write a book about them, his or her book would be a *secondary source*. A "secondary source" is derived from one or more primary sources.

At first glance, it might seem that using secondary sources is the best approach. Why go through the trouble of reading all of John Wesley's writings and sermons when someone has already done all the work for you? That's the way I used to reason—before law school.

The Problem with Secondary Sources

All of us beginning law students were required to take a course on legal research. The class was taught by a young professor named Frank Newton. He was an intellectual giant whose mind was often way ahead of ours. As part of this course, Professor Newton took us to the law school library and helped us become familiar with all of the source material available to attorneys. He showed us the primary sources: statute books and case reporters (collections of court decisions). Then he showed us the secondary sources: legal encyclopedias, textbooks, and treatises. He emphasized that we should *never* rely on these secondary sources.

"Never stop until you have gone to the primary sources," he told us. He went on to explain that secondary sources are mainly a way to find the actual court decisions and statutes. For example, if an attorney wants to know what the law is concerning animal pets, he or she will probably begin by looking in the legal encyclopedia under "Animals." The article he or she finds there will explain the law about pets and will cite the pertinent statutes and court decisions. However, the attorney can't stop there. Rather, he or she must then go and read all the actual statutes and court decisions cited. Finally, the attorney will then find and read all *other* court cases that have ever cited those statutes or decisions.

Well, as a new law student, it seemed to me that this lengthy procedure was simply busywork. After all, the articles written in the legal encyclopedias were written by attorneys and law professors. "Surely, they knew what the law was," I thought to myself. "Why re-invent the wheel? Why duplicate the research that someone else has already done?"

It wasn't very long after I had graduated from law school that the wisdom of the professor's counsel was poignantly brought home to me. A dispute had arisen over the ownership of some property, and I wasn't sure what the law was in that particular case. It was late Friday afternoon, so I quickly looked through one of the legal encyclopedias to find out what the law was. To my consternation, the information in the encyclopedia indicated that the law was squarely against my client. If we went to court, we would lose.

I started to call my client and tell him the bad news, but as it was late in the day I decided to wait until the next week. Over the weekend, I thought about Professor Newton's words and decided that I really should read the court decisions cited. So on Monday I went back and read the actual court cases that the encyclopedia had cited. To my utter amazement (and elation!), I found that the law was just the *opposite* of what the legal encyclopedia had said. The law was solidly on our side.

I was quite baffled as to how the attorney who wrote the encyclopedia article could have missed the boat by so much. The key court decision was not at all difficult to understand.

I have since learned from other attorneys that my experience was by no means unique. Legal encyclopedias are full of errors. For that reason, probably no judge would even *consider* a legal brief in which the attorney cited as his only source of authority an article from a legal encyclopedia or other secondary source.

I can assure you that the errors in legal encyclopedias are not there because the lawyers writing the articles were prejudiced or were deliberately trying to mislead their readers. The lawyers writing the articles do not care *what* the law is on a particular subject. Their only goal is to accurately and objectively report the law as it stands. Yet, they still make mistakes because they are human.

From Bad to Worse

Now, if legal secondary sources cannot be relied upon, how much less so can religious secondary sources! Not only is there the same margin for accidental error, but also there is the compounded problem of preconceived theological viewpoints. A person does not get to a position where he is asked to write articles for Bible encyclopedias or commentaries without having gone through an enormous amount of seminary or university indoctrination first. The Christian reference book writer is not a person with a blank slate who is independently seeking God's truth. Instead, he normally has some type of theological or intellectual orthodoxy that he must adhere to if he expects his work to be accepted.

Even if the writer were historically objective and spiritually honest, he still would have an editor and a publishing house over him. And editors and publishing houses have some very definite prior convictions and publishing policies. They will not normally print something that contradicts their stated positions.

The problem is further compounded by the fact that most commentaries, study Bibles, Bible dictionaries, church history books, and other Christian reference works are not, strictly speaking, *secondary* sources. Remember, our definition of a secondary source is one that is derived from one or more primary sources.

Most books that purport to give historical information about the church in the first and second centuries are based, not on primary sources, but on someone else's books. I refer to them as "tertiary" sources (tertiary meaning "third").* In other words, the writer has no firsthand knowledge of what he is discussing. He is simply relying upon the research of others, and he compounds their prejudices and errors.

Tertiary sources are the equivalent of what we refer to as hearsay in the legal world. Basically speaking, hearsay is evidence that does *not* come from a person's own firsthand knowledge. For example, someone may tell me that her neighbor gets drunk every night. Now, if I have never personally seen her neighbor drunk, my information is hearsay. It would not normally be admissible in a court of law. When we rely upon tertiary source material, we are essentially relying upon hearsay. And hearsay is never a very good basis for discovering truth.

Actually, most Christian source books, commentaries, and reference works, do not even qualify in my book as tertiary sources. That's because they are not even based upon secondary sources. Rather, the writer is relying on other tertiary sources. I refer to them as "quaternary" sources (quaternary meaning "fourth."). In other words, the author himself has never read any primary sources or even secondary sources. Instead, he has only read what other people have said, who themselves have never read any of the original sources. Although the author is very far removed from the actual sources of authority, he writes as though he *knows* what he is talking about. And people accept his word without question, particularly if he has a Ph.D. or Th.D. after his name.

The sad result is that the sheer conjecture of some seminary professor is repeated in dozens of books by various

---

*In a loose sense, all derivative books are often spoken of as "secondary" sources—even though technically they may be actually only tertiary or quaternary sources.

authors who have no way of evaluating the accuracy of his conjecture. So pretty soon what is nothing more than fanciful speculation or biased invention takes on the ring of truth because so many people are saying it. Let me give you an illustration of what I'm talking about.

I've mentioned that one of the popular understandings today of 1 Corinthians 11 is that this was simply a first century cultural problem. Paul gave his instruction about the head covering because prostitutes didn't wear head coverings, and if the Christian women weren't veiled, they would be thought of as prostitutes. I've heard that explanation dozens of times. Yet, it is not based on any historical evidence whatsoever from the writings of the early Church. It is someone's sheer conjecture. Yet it is more readily believed than is the actual light that the primary sources shed on this subject.

Principle No. 6

To find the truth about historic Christianity, you must go to the primary sources.

But I think we've talked enough about unreliable source material. Let's now look at where we *can* go to find out what the course of performance was of the New Testament Corinthian congregation—and of the other New Testament churches.

9

The Horse's Mouth

As we have said, undoubtedly the first century Corinthian congregation correctly understood what Paul was teaching them about the prayer covering. However, we are not in a position to ask those Corinthian Christians to explain Paul's letter to us. But the next generation of Corinthian Christians were. In fact, they did not have to *ask*, for they were eyewitnesses of the course of performance of the original Corinthian congregation. They saw how the original Corinthian congregation understood Paul's letter.

And they have left us a historical record of their "course of performance." This historical record extends at least as far back as A.D. 96—possibly even as far back as A.D. 60 or 70. The writings from Christians who lived before A.D. 200 are quite extensive. They are over five times as long as the New Testament writings.

These writings by no means clarify every verse of the New Testament. However, they do clearly reveal what the primitive church believed on the major doctrines: the Trinity, the Incarnation, salvation, free will, rewards and

punishments after death, baptism, the atonement, and the
Eucharist or communion. They also reveal the practice or
"course of performance" of the early church on baptism,
communion, the prayer covering, love feast, church meetings, and similar practices. They graphically describe the
lifestyle of Christians in that age, and they reveal their
understandings of virtually every commandment and moral
teaching found in the New Testament.

These writings from the first and second centuries are forti-
fied by a vast collection of writings (over ten times the size
of the New Testament) from the period between A.D. 200
and 300. Appendix A provides a list of various English
translations of the early Christian writings, so that you can
obtain and read them for yourself.

But please do not refer to these writers as the "church fathers." These men were not fathers—they were disciples.
Some of them—such as Polycarp, Ignatius, and Clement of
Rome—were personal disciples of the apostles. Others were
only one or two generations removed from the apostles.*

These men were not theological innovators. Rather, most
of them were defending Christianity against pagan and
Jewish critics, or against heretics. In their writings, they
repeatedly declared that the things they were writing were
what the whole Church believed. For example, Justin
Martyr, who wrote several apologetic works, almost always
used the term "we" in describing to the Romans and Jews
what Christians believed and practiced. He even told the
Roman emperor and senators, "And be it yours, as powerful
rulers, to inquire whether we have been taught and do truly
teach these things."[1]

---

*For an introduction to the lives and teachings of the early Christian
writers, I refer you to my earlier book, *Will The Real Heretics Please
Stand Up.*

Another example is the apologetic work, *To Diognetus,* thought to have been written about A.D. 125. Its purpose was to explain actual Christian beliefs and practices to the pagan official, Diognetus. For this official was "exceedingly desirous to learn the mode of worshipping God prevalent among the Christians, and inquiring very carefully and earnestly concerning them, what God they trust in, and what form of religion they observe."[2]

These early Christian writers repeatedly testified that the things about which they wrote were handed down to the Church by the apostles. For example, Clement of Alexandria* wrote:

> Now this work of mine in writing is not artfully constructed for display; but my memoranda are stored up against old age, as a remedy against forgetfulness, truly an image and outline of those vigorous and animated discourses which I was privileged to hear, and of blessed and truly remarkable men. . . . They preserving well the tradition of the blessed doctrine derived directly from the holy apostles, Peter, James, John, and Paul, the sons receiving it from the fathers (but few were like the fathers), came by God's will to us also to deposit those ancestral and apostolic seeds.[3]

In his work against the gnostics, written about A.D. 185, Irenaeus, bishop or overseer of the church in Lyons, France wrote:

---

*Clement of Alexandria learned the precepts of Christianity firsthand by sitting at the feet of the oldest, most respected Christian elders of his age. He eventually settled in Alexandria, Egypt, where he was made an elder and placed in charge of training new Christians.

Now the Church, although scattered over the whole civilized world to the end of the earth, received from the apostles and their disciples its faith in one God. . . . Having received this preaching and this faith, as I have said, the Church, although scattered in the whole world, carefully preserves it, as if living in one house. She believes these things [everywhere] alike, as if she had but one heart and one soul, and preaches them harmoniously, teaches them, and hands them down, as if she had but one mouth. For the languages of the world are different, but the meaning of the [apostolic] tradition is one and the same.

Neither do the churches that have been established in Germany believe otherwise, or hand down any other tradition, nor those among the Iberians, nor those among the Celts, nor in Egypt, nor in Libya, nor those established in the middle parts of the world. . . . Neither will one of those who preside in the churches who is very powerful in speech say anything different from these things, for no one is above [his] teacher, nor will one who is weak in speech diminish the tradition.[4]

"But, wasn't Irenaeus several generations removed from the apostles?" you might ask. "How could he be sure that the faith had been accurately handed down to him?" The answer is that Irenaeus was only *one* human link removed from the period of the apostles. He was a student of Polycarp, who was a personal disciple of the apostle John. Irenaeus wrote, "Similarly, Polycarp, who not only was taught by apostles, and associated with many who had seen Christ, but was installed by apostles for Asia, as bishop in the church in Smyrna—I saw him myself in my early youth—survived for a long time, and departed this life in a ripe old age by a glorious and magnificent martyrdom. He always taught what he learned from the apostles, which the Church continues to hand on, and which are the only truths."[5]

All of the works about which I am speaking were written by men who were considered orthodox by the early Church throughout the world.[*] These writers were not heretics or independent thinkers who were off in a world of their own. Most of the writers from the first two centuries were elders or bishops in the Church. Not only did their writings reflect the faith of the Church and of Scripture, but these writers also *lived* out their faith. All of them risked their lives to write on behalf of the Church, and a number of them died for their faith.

The apostles spent the greater part of the first century establishing churches and teaching correct doctrine and practice to them. I firmly believe that "the faith was once for all delivered to the saints" (Jude 3). "Jesus Christ is the same yesterday and today, *yes* and forever" (Heb. 13:8). That being the case, the faith was complete when the apostles passed it on to the next generation. The Church wasn't going to grow into a clearer and clearer understanding of true Christianity as the centuries passed. Rather, unless it held on tô what was handed down to it, there was only one direction to grow: away from Biblical Christianity.

Moreover, unlike some Christians of later centuries, the generation that received the faith directly from the apostles did not claim to have any further revelation or new light on Scripture.[6] They believed that all necessary truth had already been revealed by the apostles. They were committed to

---

[*]The writers of which I am speaking are basically the same writers who are listed as orthodox in *The Ante-Nicene Fathers*.

faithfully handing down to the next generation what they had received.

And we have a solid historical record of what that generation of Christians believed and practiced. So let's see what light they shed on the meaning of 1 Corinthians 11.

10

The Answer

Was Paul talking about a cloth veil, or was he talking about long hair? Or was there actually no custom at all about either one? The historical evidence is strikingly clear.

The record reveals that the early churches all understood Paul to be talking about a cloth veil, not long hair. The only thing that wasn't clear to some of the early Christians was whether or not Paul's instructions apply to all females or only to married women. The reason is that the Greek word *gyne,* used by Paul, can mean "a female" or it can mean "a married woman."

Around the year 200, at Carthage, North Africa, Tertullian* wrote a tract entitled, "The Veiling of Virgins," in which he argued that Paul was using the word *gyne* in the

---

*Tertullian was an elder in the North African church at Carthage and was one of the most gifted apologists of the early Church. He penned his writings during a span of about 20 years, from A.D. 190 to 210. In addition to his apologetic works, Tertullian wrote several essays, exhorting Christians to maintain their separation from the world. For more information about Tertullian and the other early Christian writers, I refer you to my earlier book, *Will The Real Heretics Please Stand Up.*

sense of "a female." In the course of his argument, Tertullian described the various practices throughout the Church, including the practice in the church at Corinth. His tract gives us a wealth of information:

> I also admonish you second group of women, who are married,[1] not to outgrow the discipline of the veil. Not even for a moment of an hour. Because you can't avoid wearing a veil, you should not find some other way to nullify it. That is, by going about neither covered nor bare. For some women do not *veil* their heads, but rather bind them up with turbans and woollen bands. It's true that they are protected in front. But where the head properly lies, they are bare.
>
> Others cover only the area of the brain with small linen coifs that do not even quite reach the ears.... They should know that the entire head constitutes the woman. Its limits and boundaries reach as far as the place where the robe begins. The region of the veil is co-extensive with the space covered by the hair when it is unbound. In this way, the neck too is encircled.
>
> The pagan women of Arabia will be your judges. For they cover not only the head, but the face also. . . . But how severe a chastisement will they likewise deserve, who remain uncovered even during the recital of the Psalms and at any mention of the name of God? For even when they are about to spend time in prayer itself, they only place a fringe, tuft [of cloth], or any thread whatever on the crown of their heads. And they think that they are covered![2]

Earlier in his tract, Tertullian testified that the churches that were founded by the apostles did insist that both their married women and their virgins be veiled:

> Throughout Greece, and certain of its barbaric provinces, the majority of churches keep their virgins covered. In fact, this practice is followed in certain places beneath this African sky. So let no one ascribe this custom merely to the Gentile customs of the Greeks and barbarians.
>
> Moreover, I will put forth as models those churches that were founded by either apostles or apostolic men. . . . The Corinthians themselves understood him to speak in this manner. For to this very day the Corinthians veil their virgins. What the apostles taught, the disciples of the apostles confirmed.[3]

Clement of Alexandria, an elder writing from Egypt around the year 190, counseled:

> "Let the woman observe this, further. Let her be entirely covered, unless she happens to be at home. For that style of dress is grave, and protects from being gazed at. And she will never fall, who puts before her eyes modesty, and her shawl; nor will she invite another to fall into sin by uncovering her face. For this is the wish of the Word, since it is becoming for her to pray veiled."[4]

Hippolytus, a leader in the church at Rome around the year 200, compiled a record of the various customs and practices in that church from the generations that preceded him. His *Apostolic Tradition* contains this statement:

"And let all the women have their heads covered
with an opaque cloth, not with a veil of thin linen,
for this is not a true covering."[5]

This written evidence of the course of performance of the
early Christians is corroborated by the archaeological record.
The pictures we have from the second and third centuries
from the catacombs and other places depict Christian women
praying with a cloth veil on their heads.[6]

So the historical record is crystal clear. It reveals that the
early generation of believers understood the head covering
to be a cloth veil—not long hair. As Tertullian indicated,
even the women who did not wish to follow Paul's teaching
were not claiming that Paul was talking about long hair.
Rather, they simply wore a small cloth in minimal obedience
to his teaching. *Nobody* in the early Church claimed that
Paul's instructions were merely a concession to Greek
culture. *Nobody* claimed that they had anything to do with
prostitutes or pagan priestesses.

Back to Scripture

Now, let's go back to Scripture, and see if the historical
understanding is based upon a reasonable interpretation of
the Scriptures. The early Christian understanding of this
passage gives the full literal meaning to verse 4 (a man must
not wear anything on his head when praying or prophesying)
and to verse 5 (a woman should be veiled or covered when
praying or prophesying). Yet, it does not contradict verses
14 and 15 that nature teaches us the same principle that men
should not be veiled but that women should, since men naturally wear their hair short and women wear it long.

More importantly, the historic record nicely fits the final common sense rule of interpretation we attorneys use. The American Law Institute has expressed this principle as follows: "An interpretation which gives a reasonable, lawful, and effective meaning to *all* the terms is preferred to an interpretation which leaves a part unreasonable, unlawful, or of no effect."[7]

Applying this principle to Bible interpretation, we can state it this way:

Principle No. 7

An interpretation that leaves parts of Scripture void or unreasonable should be rejected.

This principle is simply common sense reduced to words. When you or I write a letter or an essay, we normally intend for everything we write to have meaning, don't we? We don't intend for some of our statements to be totally ignored. Nor do we intend for part of what we write to be interpreted in such a way as to totally nullify the other things we have written.

The historical interpretation of 1 Corinthians 11 squarely meets this common sense principle. It gives full meaning to everything Paul has said. In contrast, our modern interpretations do not. Take, for example, the interpretation that Paul was saying that men should wear their hair short and women should wear their hair long. What does it do to verses 4 through 6? Paul says in verse 4: "Every man who has *something* on his head while praying or prophesying, disgraces his head." Under this interpretation, the "something" that Paul is talking about would have to be hair, wouldn't it? So should men shave off all of their hair?

In verse 6, Paul says, "If a woman does not cover her head, let her also have her hair cut off." To follow the modern interpretation, Paul would be saying, "If a woman does not have long hair, let her also have her hair cut off." How reasonable is that? If a woman's hair is short, it is because it is already cut off.

If Paul is talking about the length of hair, why would he focus on "praying or prophesying"? Can a man's hair be long while he is doing other things and then suddenly become short when he is praying or prophesying? Can a woman's hair be short while she is doing other things and then suddenly become long when she is praying or prophesying?

In short, this modern interpretation reduces most of this passage to an absurdity. If Paul were simply addressing the length of hair, why didn't he just come out and say it? Why would he have gone through this protracted language about coverings or veils? He could have simply said, "Men should wear their hair short and women should wear their hair long." Any interpretation that renders a passage absurd is an absurd interpretation.

Or how about the interpretation that the only reason that this passage was written was so that the Christian women of Corinth wouldn't be mistaken as prostitutes or pagan priestesses? If that is what this passage is all about, why is part of it addressed to men? Furthermore this interpretation contradicts what Paul said in verse ten: "Therefore the woman ought to have a symbol of authority on her head, *because of the angels*." If this modern interpretation were correct, then Paul is either in error here or else he is lying. In other words, either Paul didn't know why he was giving these instructions (mistakenly thinking that they had something to do with the angels), or else he purposely gave a false reason. In short, this interpretation fails the test of common sense, for it invalidates most of what Paul said.

Another modern interpretation is even worse. This is the interpretation that verse sixteen is saying that there was no such custom of wearing a head covering. "But if one is inclined to be contentious, we have no other practice, nor have the churches of God." Was Paul saying, "There is no other practice than to be unveiled"? Or was he saying, "There is no other practice than to be veiled"? If we say that Paul was saying that there is no other practice than to be unveiled, then why did Paul even bother to write this passage at all? In effect, we have him giving all of this counsel, connecting it to the order of creation and to the angels, and then saying, "But if you don't like these instructions, don't follow them, for no one else is following them either."

The Excellence of the Historic Interpretations

In contrast, the historic understanding offers us a literal, reasonable interpretation of the aforementioned passage. Every other interpretation ends up nullifying all or part of it. Some interpretations also add a lot of assumptions that aren't even in the passage.

I have found this same pattern to be true of all of the early Christian understandings of Scripture. They don't *add* something to Scripture; they *take away* the human traditions that we have added. They nearly always leave us with the bare, literal meaning of Scripture. They bring us back to the meaning we would have seen to start with if we had not been blinded by our preconceptions.

As I said previously, this is not a book about the head covering. We have been looking at the passage in 1 Corinthi-

ans 11 only to illustrate this common sense approach to
Scripture interpretation. So let's review these common sense
principles:

The Seven Common Sense Principles of Scripture Interpretation

1. Begin with a blank slate.

2. Start at the beginning of the New Testament, with the teachings of Jesus.

3. Give each verse its literal meaning.

4. Consider every Scripture that relates, or could relate, to the subject.

5. Reject any interpretation that would render some of the Scriptures void or unreasonable.

6. Look at the "course of performance": how the first several generations of Christians understood the Scripture.

7. To determine the "course of performance," always go to the primary sources.

It's that easy. In fact, it's almost *too* easy. It's so obvious,
why have Christians not been using it? Why on earth have
we Protestants torn asunder the Body of Christ so needless-
ly? I can assure you that it isn't because no one else has ever
thought of looking at the historic course of performance.
Rather, it's because those who have searched the historical
record have not found what they *wanted* to find!

11

The Big Surprise

My father was in the Air Force, and I grew up on military bases. As a result, we were rarely able to have a garden. So I grew up never having eaten a vine-ripened tomato. Instead, all of the tomatoes I ever ate as a child had come from a grocery store. They had been picked green, and sat in their bin at the market in a motley coat of green, pink, and light red. Their flesh was a pinkish, light red and was quite firm. In fact it was almost crunchy—like a cucumber. And I liked them! As far as I knew, this is what a *real* tomato was supposed to be like.

One day, after I had left home, some friends invited me over to their house for lunch. They were country folks, and a hefty portion of our lunch came out of their garden. Sitting right in the middle of the table was a plate of sliced garden-fresh, vine-ripened tomatoes. I eyed them with suspicion. There they were—a deep blood red. Not at all the color that tomatoes are supposed to be. I suspected they must be rotten.

Yet, being a hungry, skinny kid of eighteen, I wasn't about to offend my hosts (and miss out on being invited back some time), so I politely placed some of the tomato slices on my plate when they were passed to me. Feeling as if all eyes were focused on me, I gingerly inserted a slice of those strange-looking tomatoes in my mouth. As I played around with the piece of tomato on my tongue, I noticed uncomfortably that it practically dissolved in my mouth. It wasn't at all crunchy like a tomato was supposed to be. It didn't even taste right.

"These definitely are rotten," I thought to myself. "I'm sure glad I wasn't raised in the country and forced to eat rotten tomatoes like these poor country people."

Slowly, over a period of several years, I finally came to realize that those "rotten" tomatoes were actually what real tomatoes are supposed to taste like. What I had grown up with was far from the real thing. In fact, I eventually came to enjoy vine-ripened tomatoes so much that I now dislike having to eat the store-bought kind. My wife and I are not big gardeners, but every place we live, we always have at least a small plot with fresh, vine-ripened tomatoes.

When it comes to Christianity, we have all grown up with the "store-bought" kind. It is all we have ever known, and we have grown accustomed to it. To us, real Christianity should taste, look, and feel like the kind *we* have. So when we first come face-to-face with genuine, primitive, "vine-ripened" Christianity, it doesn't look right to us. It doesn't taste like we want it to taste. And unless we are driven by deep spiritual hunger, we quickly reject it and go back to our store-bought variety.

Get Ready For A Shock

I think the biggest shock to all of us Protestant or evangelical Christians when we read the early Christian writings is the discovery that the Reformation was no return to primitive Christianity. Many of the cardinal doctrines of the Reformers do not find any support at all in the historical record of early Christianity.

In fact, probably *everyone* who reads the early Christian writings today finds that some of his or her beliefs are not supported by the historic record—regardless of what denomination he or she belongs to. At the same time, everyone finds that some of his or her beliefs are precisely what the Church taught in its early years. In fact, some groups find that most of their beliefs are the same. But most of us don't. I found that only about half of my beliefs matched theirs.

But that's not the only jolt we receive. Most of us also discover that the early Christians weren't at all like we had imagined. That's because we have so westernized, modernized, "Protestantized," and sanitized the apostles that we take them out of their historical setting. When we are transported back to their real-life setting, we find a Christianity that is often strikingly different from ours.

Let me tell you some of the things I'm talking about. First of all, you will find that the second century Christians did not have a twentieth century knowledge of science and medicine. You will also discover that the early Church used the Septuagint as their Old Testament, rather than the Masoretic text.* You will learn that they sometimes quote

---

*The Masoretic text is the Hebrew text type of the Old Testament that became standardized and recognized as authoritative by the Jews after the fall of Jerusalem in A.D. 70. It became the uniform text used by Jews and Roman Catholics during the Middle Ages. The Septuagint was the

from spiritual books that most of us have never read—like Enoch and the Wisdom of Solomon. You will find that they see in the Mosaic Law various spiritual truths that we would have never thought of. And not only will you discover that many of their beliefs and practices are different from ours, you'll also discover that their whole pattern of reasoning is often different. In fact, sometimes their logic just doesn't make sense to us.

But perhaps what offends us the most about early Christianity is that it was a Christianity that *crucified* the flesh, rather than indulging it. It was a Christianity far removed from today's gospel of "easy believism."

What Should Our Response Be?

So what should our response be to all of these "strange" things? I can tell you what my initial response was: I quit reading the early Christian writings. After a couple evenings of reading *The Ante-Nicene Fathers*, I just said to myself, "That's it. These guys are way off base, and I don't need to listen to any more of them." I pitched the volumes of their writings back on my library shelf, and I tried to simply dismiss them from my mind.

I believe that it was the prompting of the Holy Spirit that made me go back to them. So a few months later, I gave them another chance. This time I began with a different writer than I had the first time. But the results were the same. "This can't be right," I kept saying over and over to

---

first translation made of the Old Testament into Greek. It is our primary witness of an older text type used by many Jews in the 2nd and 3rd centuries B. C. The Septuagint was the primary Old Testament version used by the early Christians, and it has remained the Old Testament text used by the eastern Christian churches down through today.

myself. "The early Church couldn't have been like this." I disappointedly shoved the books back on the shelf, and I decided again to call it quits.

Yet, I eventually came to realize that I could not change the truth about historic Christianity by ignoring the evidence. Whether I discovered what the early Christians believed or not, their beliefs were still there. I couldn't change them by closing my eyes to them. I realized that I owed it to myself and my family to find out what primitive Christianity was *really* like.

So the third time, I approached these historic writings with a different attitude. The first two times, I had continually argued with them as I read, saying things such as, "No, you can't mean that!" Or, "Didn't you guys read what Paul said?" And on and on.

This time I realized that if I was ever going to find out how the second generation of Christians understood the apostles, I was going to have to temporarily set aside everything that I believed—and just listen. I knew I was under no obligation to adopt their doctrines. But I owed it to myself to honestly know *what* those doctrines were. "When it's all over," I reasoned, "I'll still be free to take back all of my present beliefs."

So I began reading with a different frame of mind. This time, I just listened to what they had to say, rather than arguing with them. Gradually, I became used to their way of thinking. Finally, after reading their writings every evening for about six months, I was overwhelmed with a thirst to go back and read the New Testament again. So I did. In a couple of evenings, I read the whole New Testament, gulping in its spiritual waters.

I had previously read the New Testament dozens of times, from beginning to end. But as I read it this time, something was marvelously different. I noticed all sorts of statements in Scripture that I had never seen before. My eyes were opened to verse after verse that had formerly been hidden from me. More importantly, I noticed an incredible similarity between the teachings and thought patterns of the New Testament writers and those of the second century Christians.

I suddenly realized how my eyes and ears had been closed to so many things in Scripture all of my life. I perceived how much we have westernized, modernized, and *sanitized* the New Testament. Most of the things I found strange in the early Christian writings had been in the New Testament all along. I simply had never noticed them. Let me illustrate.

12

The Forgotten Septuagint

The Septuagint was the first translation made of the Hebrew Old Testament into Greek. It was begun over two hundred years before the birth of Jesus. It often reads differently from the Masoretic text, the Old Testament text that became standardized for the Jews after A.D. 70.* Since most Old Testaments used today in the West have been translated from the Masoretic text, it means that the early Christian quotations from the Old Testament sometimes do not fit our Bibles.

As I have mentioned, at first it seemed strange to me that the early Christians preferred the Septuagint—a translation—over the Hebrew text of their day. Yet, how could I have been so blind to the fact that most of the New Testament writers, too, preferred the Septuagint over the Masoretic-type Hebrew texts of their day? When they quoted from the Old Testament, the apostles primarily quoted from

---

*With the exception of the prophecy about the virgin birth of Jesus, which is discussed herein, these textual differences do not affect any essential teachings of Christianity.

the Septuagint. So *their* quotations, too, frequently don't match the Old Testament passages in our Bibles.

For example, notice this passage from the Psalms that is quoted in the Book of Hebrews: "Therefore, when He comes into the world, He says, 'Sacrifice and offering thou hast not desired, but a body thou hast prepared for me'" (Heb. 10:5,6). However, the Masoretic text of Psalm 40:6 says, "Sacrifice and meal offering Thou hast not desired; my ears Thou hast opened."

Our Bibles don't say anything in Psalms about "a body Thou hast prepared for me." Is that not part of Scripture? If it isn't, why did the writer of Hebrews quote it as Scripture?

That is not an isolated example. Such variances between the Septuagint and the Masoretic text are fairly numerous. In fact, one of the cardinal teachings of Christianity turns on one of these variances. We have all read Matthew's quotation from Isaiah 7:14: "Now all this took place that what was spoken by the Lord through the prophet might be fulfilled, saying, 'Behold, the virgin shall be with child, and shall bear a Son, and they shall call His name Immanuel'" (Matt. 1:22,23). What I did not realize until recently was that the Hebrew Masoretic text does not say, "the *virgin* shall be with child." It says, "the *young woman* shall be with child." No wonder the apostles and their disciples chose the Septuagint over the Masoretic text.

Unless you use the Revised Standard Version, if you look up Isaiah 7:14 in your Old Testament, you will probably find that it reads "virgin" instead of "young woman." That's because translators have fudged on their use of the Masoretic text in order to conform to the cardinal Christian doctrine of the virgin birth. But how honest is that? Can we ignore the Septuagint and treat it as "a translation full of errors," but then when one of those "errors" supports a major Christian doctrine, go over and borrow from it? Are we really seeking truth when we do that?

Is the Septuagint Full of Errors?

During the Middle Ages, and for many centuries thereafter, western Christians mistakenly thought that the Septuagint was merely a careless translation of the Hebrew text. Many Christians today still think that. I know that's what I believed until recently. However, during the 1800s, scholars began to postulate that perhaps the reason for the variance between the Septuagint and the Masoretic text was that the translators of the Septuagint were working from an earlier Hebrew text that varied from the later Masoretic text.

In 1947, when scholars were still speculating about these things, an Arab shepherd accidentally discovered some ancient Jewish scrolls near the settlement of Qumran in Palestine. Those scrolls, along with numerous other scrolls later found in the same vicinity, have come to be known as the Dead Sea Scrolls, or the Qumran Library. The Old Testament texts found among these scrolls were centuries older than any previously known Old Testament manuscripts. Among the first scrolls examined were two manuscripts of the Book of Isaiah. The initial published reports proclaimed that those manuscripts were virtually identical to the Masoretic text of today. Evangelical Christians were quick to propagate these initial reports. I remember reading such reports myself and spreading them to others.

However, later, a more sober reflection on the Isaiah scrolls, coupled with the discovery of Dead Sea manuscripts for other Old Testament books, revealed that the initial reports were premature. Rather than vindicating the Masoretic text as being *the* original Hebrew text, the thousands of Qumran text specimens reveal that there was a definite diversity of text types of the Old Testament in use during the centuries before Christ. The Masoretic text reflects only *one* of those text types. Unfortunately, evangelicals have not been very quick to retract those original premature reports.

More importantly, those manuscripts confirmed that there were early Hebrew manuscripts that largely agree textually with the Septuagint. So the Septuagint was not a sloppy translation of the Masoretic text. Rather, it is apparently a reasonably faithful translation of another text type—a text that may well be older than the prototype of the Masoretic text. Again, let me emphasize that the differences between these text types do not affect any significant spiritual truths. They mainly affect the wording of various Old Testament passages.

The Value of the Septuagint

More and more Bible scholars today are recognizing the immense value of the Septuagint and its unique relationship to the New Testament. For example, Bible scholar George Howard points out:

> If the writers of the NT [New Testament] were influenced by secular Greek, they were influenced more by LXX [Septuagint]. Separated from LXX the NT would have been almost unintelligible to the contemporary reader, according to B. Atkinson. ...
> At any rate, in the past decades there has developed an appreciation for the influence which LXX vocabulary had on NT thought and the contributions in this area of Septuagintal research are still coming. Consequently, the debate over which source is more

important for NT lexicography, Greek or Hebrew, will probably be resolved in terms of LXX.[1]

Dr. Sven Soderlund of Regent College writes:

> The LXX was the Bible for most writers of the NT. Not only did they take from it most of their express citations of Scripture, but their writings—in particular the Gospels, and among them especially Luke—contain numerous reminiscences of its language. The theological terms of the NT, such as "law," "righteousness," "mercy," "truth," "propitiation," were taken over directly from the LXX and must be understood in the light of their use in that version.[2]

Other Old Testament scholars have expressed similar sentiments.*

Although the vindication of the Septuagint may come as a surprise to many western Christians, it doesn't surprise the eastern churches at all. That's because the Septuagint has

---

*For instance, Old Testament scholar Dikran Y. Hadidian writes: "F. W. Danker in his article on 'Aids to Bible Study; The Septuagint—its History,' refers to the remark by the eminent Biblical critic and Hebraist, Ferdinand Hitzig, to his students: 'Gentlemen, have you a Septuagint? If not, sell all you have, and buy a Septuagint.' E. Stauffer gives the answer as to why a man ought to sell all his possessions and buy a Septuagint: ...'*The OT [Old Testament] was the Bible of primitive Christianity.*What the writers of the NT [New Testament] read in the OT became the normal starting point for their own formulation of ideas....The writers of the NT were deeply versed in the LXX [Septuagint], its language, its text, and its textual tradition. This is adequate ground for us to take the LXX as our constant aid in understanding the NT, and in the main to use the Greek Text for OT references.'"[3]

always been their Old Testament—from the days of the apostles to the modern day. The Eastern and the Oriental Orthodox Churches did not need to wait for archaeological findings to support the Septuagint. Rather, the only evidence they ever needed was the fact the Septuagint was the Bible of the New Testament Church.

However, the use of the Septuagint is not the only spiritual bombshell that hits us when we read the early Christian works.

13

Other Bombshells

When I first came across a quotation from the Apocrypha in the early Christian writings, I nearly fell off of my sofa. "This can't be!" I thought to myself. "The Apocrypha is something the Roman Catholic Church added to Scripture. How can a second century Christian be quoting from it?"

Well, before long I found several quotations from what we Protestants call the "Apocrypha." Actually, the quotations from the Apocrypha should not have surprised me. For those writings were simply part of the Septuagint of the New Testament period. From the evidence of the early Christian writings, it appears that they were almost universally accepted as Scripture by the early Church. It was not until the fourth century that Jerome gave these works the epithet, "Apocrypha."

I was quite surprised to eventually learn that the writings of the Apocrypha were originally included in the King James Version of the Bible. However, they were preceded by a comment that they were not considered authoritative for doctrine. It was not until 1827 that they generally disappeared from printed copies of the King James Bible.[1]

The work from the Apocrypha from which the early Christians quote most often is the Book of Wisdom, also called the Wisdom of Solomon. The early Christians understood this book to be primarily speaking about Christ, the eternal Word or Logos of the Father. In doing so, they were apparently following the example of the apostles.

Although there are no word-for-word quotations from the Book of Wisdom in the New Testament, there appear to be many paraphrased quotations from it and references to it. For example, the attributes of the Person called "Wisdom" in the Book of Wisdom closely resemble the New Testament descriptions of the Son of God. In fact, Paul specifically referred to Christ as "the power of God and the *wisdom* of God" (1 Cor. 1:24, italics mine). Furthermore, the Book of Wisdom describes the Divine Wisdom as the "reflection of the everlasting light, and a spotless mirror of the activity of God, and a likeness of his goodness" (Wis. 7:26 Gsp). In similar language, Hebrews describes Christ as "the radiance of His glory and the exact representation of His nature" (Heb. 1:3).

What's more, the general theology of Wisdom is remarkably similar to that of the New Testament. And there are at least thirty passages in the New Testament that are direct parallels to verses in the Wisdom of Solomon. One example is Romans 9:21, "Does not the potter have a right over the clay, to make from the same lump one vessel for honorable use, and another for common use?" Although our Bibles usually cite Jeremiah 18:3 as the source of Paul's words, I think it is much more likely that Paul was paraphrasing Wisdom 15:7 : "For truly the potter, laboriously working the soft earth, molds for our service each several article: Both the vessels that serve for clean purposes and their opposites, all alike. As to what shall be the use of each vessel of either class, the worker in clay is the judge."*

Are we to believe that the many parallel passages between Wisdom and the New Testament are just coincidences? Is the similarity between Wisdom theology and Christian theology just an accident? If the Book of Wisdom is the work of a mere human author, how did that author obtain such spiritual insight?

So what am I getting at? I'm primarily saying that, if we are going to understand the Scriptures the way the New Testament Christians understood them, we need to familiarize ourselves with the same spiritual works that they were reading. Not that we are going to find new doctrines or

---

*Other examples of parallel passages are: "For indeed while we are in this tent, we groan, being burdened, because we do not want to be unclothed, but to be clothed, in order that what is mortal may be swallowed up by life" (2 Cor. 5:4). Compare this to Wisdom 9:15,16: "For the corruptible body burdens the soul and the earthen shelter weighs down the mind that has many concerns. And scarce do we guess the things on earth, and what is within our grasp we find with difficulty; but when things are in heaven, who can search them out?" In describing the reward the righteous will receive, Wisdom states, "Therefore shall they receive the splendid crown, the beauteous diadem, from the hand of the Lord" (Wis. 5:16). Paul was probably quoting from Wisdom when he told Timothy, "In the future there is laid up for me the crown of righteousness, which the Lord, the righteous Judge, will award to me on that day" (2 Tim. 4:8). Hundreds of years before Paul wrote to the Romans, Wisdom had stated: "By the envy of the devil, death entered the world, and they who are in his possession experience it" (Wis. 2:24). This corresponds to Paul's words, "Therefore, just as through one man sin entered into the world, and death through sin, and so death spread to all men, because all sinned" (Rom. 5:12). Some other parallels are: Wis. 1:4/Rom. 7:14; Wis. 1:13/2 Pet. 3:9; Wis. 2:18/Matt. 27:43; Wis. 3:7/Matt. 13:43; Wis. 5:18-20/Eph. 6:13-17; Wis. 6:1-4/Rom. 13:1-4; Wis. 9:9/John 1:1,10; Wis. 14:22-31/Rom. 1:20-32; Wis. 15:3/John 17:3; Wis. 18:15,16/Rev. 19:13,15; and Wis. 16:13/Acts 2:31.

commandments in those works, but that the works of the Apocrypha are important background sources for the New Testament.

Is the Apocrypha Scripture?

I'm also saying that we Protestants need to take a whole new look at the Apocrypha. Prominent evangelical leaders such as Josh McDowell still refer to the Apocrypha as "books added to the Old Testament by the Catholic church."[2] But nothing could be further from the truth. These weren't books that the Roman Catholics *added* to Scripture; they were books that the Jewish religious leaders *took out* of Scripture. The debates about the Apocrypha in the second century were between the Christians, who accepted these writings as Scripture, and the unbelieving Jews, who did not.[3]

Although I would by no means be dogmatic about it, I think it is quite likely that the Apostle Paul was expressly stating that these works were inspired by God when he wrote Timothy, "All Scripture is inspired by God and profitable for teaching, for reproof, for correction, for training in righteousness" (2 Tim. 3:16). What "Scripture" was Paul referring to? Why, to the same "sacred writings" that Timothy knew from childhood (2 Tim. 3:15). And what writings would they have been? Let's see.

Timothy was apparently a native of Lystra, a town in the Roman province of Galatia (Acts 16:1). His father was a Greek, and his mother was a Hellenistic Jew (Acts 16:1; 2 Tim. 1:5). So, almost beyond doubt, the "sacred writings" that Timothy had read from childhood would have been the Septuagint. That was *the* Bible of the Greek-speaking Jews. Furthermore, Paul had just finished quoting Numbers 16:5 from the Septuagint to Timothy: "The Lord knows those who are His" (2 Tim. 2:19). (The Masoretic text of Num. 16:5 reads, "The Lord will show who is His.") So when Paul spoke of "all Scripture," Timothy would naturally have understood him to be speaking of the Septuagint.

And the Septuagint of the first century contained the various books that Protestants now call the Apocrypha. Those books weren't lumped together in one section of the Septuagint, as though they somehow stood apart from the rest of the Old Testament. Rather, they were scattered throughout the Old Testament, being placed in whatever section of the Old Testament they would naturally fit, whether it was in the historical, prophetic, or poetical writings.

So when Paul said that *"all* Scripture" is inspired, wouldn't Timothy have naturally understood him to be speaking about *all* of the works contained in the Septuagint? That this is apparently the case is supported by the "course of performance" of the early Church, for they almost universally accepted the Apocrypha as inspired.

The Closing of the Jewish Canon

The writings of the Apocrypha were not officially shut out of the Jewish canon until the close of the first century. There is no doubt in my mind that the Jewish religious leaders rejected those works primarily because Christians were using them so successfully to convict the Jews. For example, the descriptions of the heavenly Son of God in the Book of Wisdom were too obvious to ignore.

Furthermore, could those religious leaders deny that the Book of Wisdom had prophesied about Jesus and his confrontation with their forefathers, the scribes and Pharisees, when it said:

He professes to have knowledge of God and styles himself a child of the Lord. To us he is the censure of our thoughts; merely to see him is a hardship for us, because his life is not like other men's, and different are his ways. He judges us debased; he holds aloof from our paths as from things impure. He calls blest the destiny of the just and boasts that God is his Father. Let us see whether his words be true; let us find out what will happen to him. For if the just one be the son of God, He will defend him and deliver him from the hand of his foes. With revilement and torture let us put him to the test that we may have proof of his gentleness and try his patience. Let us condemn him to a shameful death (Wis. 2:13-20).

That's an incredible prophecy! No wonder the scribes didn't want the Jews to read from that book anymore! And since that book was part of the Septuagint, is it any wonder that the Jewish leaders quickly dumped the entire Septuagint as well?

Who were these Jewish leaders who effectively closed the Book of Wisdom and the other books of the Apocrypha out of the Old Testament canon? Why, none others than the spiritual sons of the scribes and Pharisees, whom Jesus called "blind guides," "fools," "hypocrites," "whitewashed tombs," and the "sons of those who murdered the prophets" (Matt. 23:13-31). These were the very same men who murdered and imprisoned the early Christians.

Do we Protestants realize what we have been doing? In the selection of our Old Testament canon and text, we have been siding with the unbelieving scribes and Pharisees—the "brood of vipers"—against our faithful Christian brothers and sisters of the first and second centuries. What bitter irony! Maybe it is we who are the blind guides!

Enoch and the Assumption of Moses

You probably don't feel like being hit with any more bombshells. I didn't either. But since I've told you this much, I might as well tell you the rest. The early Christians also cited Jewish spiritual writings that were not even part of the Septuagint. In particular, they often mentioned the Book of Enoch and sometimes quoted from it. Many of the early Christians even viewed Enoch as part of Scripture, although it was not universally accepted as such.

Today, Protestants generally refer to Enoch as being part of the "Old Testament Pseudepigrapha." However, what we Protestants call the "Old Testament Pseudepigrapha" is actually a loose amalgamation of Jewish and pseudo-Jewish spiritual writings. It is inaccurate to think of these writings as though they are a related group of works, for they are not all on the same level spiritually. Some of these works, such as Enoch, contain genuine revelation from God. Others, such as the Martyrdom of Isaiah, contain apparently accurate historical information. Others, such as the Apocalypse of Adam, are evidently fictitious. The only thing these works have in common is that none of them were part of the Septuagint.

One day, over a cup of tea, I was talking with a Christian friend about the early Christian use of the Apocrypha and Pseudepigrapha. He retorted: "Well, the New Testament writers never quoted from the Apocrypha and the Pseudepigrapha, so the early Christians shouldn't have either."

"Do you accept the Book of Esther?" I asked him.

"Of course!" he replied. "It's part of Scripture."

"But the New Testament writers never quoted from it, either. And besides, it was a disputed book in the days of Jesus."

He had no reply.

"Well, would you accept the Apocrypha or Pseude-pigrapha if the New Testament writers quoted from them?" I asked him.

"Oh, yes, of course," he replied.

I then had my friend turn with me to the Book of Jude. We read together verses 14 and 15: "And about these also Enoch, *in* the seventh *generation* from Adam, prophesied, saying, 'Behold, the Lord came with many thousands of His holy ones, to execute judgment upon all, and to convict all the ungodly of all their ungodly deeds which they have done in an ungodly way, and of all the harsh things which ungodly sinners have spoken against Him.'"

"Those verses," I explained, "are a direct quotation from the Book of Enoch. So are you now willing to accept the Book of Enoch as Scripture?"

He was speechless.

Yet, Enoch is not the only work referenced in Jude. In verse 9, Jude wrote: "But Michael the archangel, when he disputed with the devil and argued about the body of Moses, did not dare pronounce against him a railing judgment, but said, 'The Lord rebuke you.'" Do you recall ever reading anything in the Old Testament about Michael and Satan arguing over the body of Moses? Of course not, because no such dispute is recorded in our Old Testament. Rather, this event is described in a work entitled the Assumption of Moses.

These quotations from Enoch and the Assumption of Moses throw an interesting wrench into our sanitized Protestant package. The term "pseudepigrapha" means writings falsely ascribed to someone other than the real author. Yet, Jude specifically said that the prophecy he quoted was from "Enoch, in the seventh generation from

Adam." So either the New Testament has an error in it, or we should not label Enoch as part of the Pseudepigrapha.

And what about the account concerning Michael's dispute with Satan? That's not something that a mere human could know anything about, is it? So the Assumption of Moses must contain some sort of revelation from God that is not in our Old Testament.

And it's not just the Book of Jude that contains references to other spiritual writings. In his second letter to Timothy, Paul wrote, "And just as Jannes and Jambres opposed Moses, so these *men* also oppose the truth" (2 Tim. 3:8). Do you recall anything in the Old Testament about some men named Jannes and Jambres, who opposed Moses? There *is* no such reference. Instead, their names appear in the Book of Jannes and Jambres. Finally, the writer of Hebrews was apparently referencing a book called the Martyrdom of Isaiah when he spoke of men of faith who had been "sawn in two" (Heb. 11:37).

"Sanitizing" the New Testament

Those spiritual writings from which the New Testament writers quoted, or to which they alluded, were widely circulated in the first century. Since the New Testament writers referred to those works, is it any wonder that the first and second century Christians were comfortable in doing the same? Why should we be surprised to find that the early Christians read and quoted from the same sources as did the New Testament writers? Yet, it does surprise us. It comes as a big surprise.

That's because we have "sanitized" the apostles by taking them out of their real-life setting. All the things in the New Testament that don't fit into our neat, trim, Protestant package, we simply attribute to "inspiration," so we can ignore them. We contend that it was all right for the apostles to refer to those works *only* because the apostles were inspired. But that's a spiritual cop-out.

Because of our Protestant biases, we have closed our eyes to some very important Jewish spiritual and historical writings—such as the Martyrdom of Isaiah and the Book of Jannes and Jambres. These are not part of Scripture, but they give background information about Scripture. We Protestants seem to think that, just because an ancient Jewish writing is not part of Scripture, it is therefore something fictitious or heretical. Would the apostles and disciples have referred to and quoted from these writings if they were fictitious or heretical?

I'm sure that I will receive an unbelievable amount of flak and denunciations for even having pointed out these things. But what would you rather that I had done? Sweep these things under the rug? Pretend I never saw them? I have brought up these matters for two reasons: First, to prepare you for what you will find when reading the early Christian writings. Secondly, to emphasize that if we are going to understand Scripture the way the New Testament Christians did, we must be familiar with the same spiritual works that they read.

Whether or not you or I accept the Apocrypha, or Enoch, as canonical is peripheral to this discussion. Our view of these works is not going to alter our Christian lifestyles. No Christian doctrines, ordinances, or commandments turn on the issue of whether or not these works should be viewed as Scripture. But let's at least be honest about these works and recognize that the apostles and early Christians used them. Let's quit closing our eyes to early Christian history.

Unfortunately, these are not the only things to which we have closed our eyes.

14

What We
Would Rather Not See

I was recently browsing through a Christian bookstore, when I noticed one or two books concerning the dangerous spread of "eastern religions." "How incredibly blind we western Christians are!" I thought to myself. "Christianity *is* an eastern religion."* And we will never be able to get into the mindset of the apostles and New Testament Christians until we recognize this.

Rudyard Kipling wrote the often-quoted words, "East is East and West is West, and never the twain shall meet."[1] Without a doubt, eastern thinking often stands in stark contrast to western rationalism. The eastern mind is much quicker than its western counterpart to grasp allegorical

---

*I am *not* saying that we shouldn't be concerned about the spread of pagan eastern religions. I'm only saying that Christianity is an eastern religion, too.

truths that are prefigured by actual historical events. The eastern mind will often believe incomprehensible spiritual truths that the western, rationalistic mind rejects.

Another difference is the western tendency towards legalism. The genius of the Romans (who were westerners) was law. Their legal system was far superior to any of the Gentile legal systems that preceded them. Our modern day law used in the western hemisphere is still largely based on Roman law. Naturally enough, western theologians have tended to conceive of Christian truths in terms of legal theories. Augustine's theology of salvation and Anselm's theology of the atonement are prime examples of western theology that reduces God's arrangements to legal principles.

But if we are to accurately understand Scripture, we must learn to think as easterners. And that's not easy for us to do. It is the eastern thinking of the early Christians that so often repulses the uninitiated western reader. He finds himself muttering, "These people don't think like I do! Their logic doesn't make any sense to me." So he quickly dismisses both them and their writings as strange.

However, the New Testament writers followed the same "peculiar logic" as did the second century Christians. If we hadn't already westernized and sanitized the New Testament, we would be able to see that. But as it is, our eyes are safely closed to the eastern way of thinking that is woven all throughout the pages of the New Testament. But since the early Christian writers have not been westernized and sanitized, we immediately notice their eastern thought process when we read their works.

Eastern Thinking in the New Testament

"Eastern thinking in the New Testament? Where?" you might be saying. Well, a person doesn't have to go very far into the New Testament before he is already waist-deep in it. For example, after describing how Joseph and Mary fled to Egypt, Matthew wrote, "[He] was there until the death of Herod, that what was spoken by the Lord through the prophet might be fulfilled, saying, 'Out of Egypt did I call My Son'" (Matt. 2:15).

"What's illogical about that?" you may be thinking. Let's turn to the passage that Matthew quoted from the Old Testament, and you will see. His quotation is from the eleventh chapter of Hosea: "When Israel *was* a youth I loved him, and out of Egypt I called My son. The more they called them, the more they went from them; they kept sacrificing to the Baals and burning incense to idols. Yet it is I who taught Ephraim to walk, I took them in My arms; But they did not know that I healed them, I led them with cords of a man, with bonds of love, and I became to them as one who lifts the yoke from their jaws; and I bent down *and* fed them. They will not return to the land of Egypt; But Assyria—he will be their king, because they refused to return *to Me*" (Hos. 11:1-5).

That's a prophecy about Jesus? It would seem to any of us that the passage from Hosea is clearly talking about the nation of Israel—not about the Messiah. Yet, I believe that Matthew did not misapply this Scripture. His reasoning is simply different than ours.

And that's no isolated example. Just a few verses down, Matthew described the slaughter of the male infants in Bethlehem, and then said, "Then that which was spoken through Jeremiah the prophet was fulfilled, saying, 'A voice was heard in Ramah, weeping and great mourning, Rachel weeping for her children; and she refused to be comforted, because they were no more'" (Matt. 15:18).

Again, let's look at what Jeremiah wrote: "'A voice is heard in Ramah, lamentation *and* bitter weeping. Rachel is weeping for her children; she refuses to be comforted for her children, because they are no more.' Thus says the Lord, 'Restrain your voice from weeping, and your eyes from tears; for your work shall be rewarded,' declares the Lord, 'and they shall return from the land of the enemy. And there is hope for your future,' declares the Lord, 'And *your* children shall return to their own territory'" (Jer. 31:15-17).

That's talking about the slaughter of the infants in Bethlehem after the birth of Jesus? The whole context of that prophecy seems to clearly be speaking of Israel's captivity and return to their land. Yet, again, I believe that Matthew was not misapplying this prophecy.

Or how about Matthew 2:22,23: "And being warned *by God* in a dream, he departed for the regions of Galilee, and came and resided in a city called Nazareth, that what was spoken through the prophets might be fulfilled, 'He shall be called a Nazarene.'" Spoken by the prophets? Where? I've heard at least three different explanations of what Matthew might have been referring to. The truth is, we simply don't know.

The point is that Matthew doesn't reason the same way we twentieth century westerners do. "But Matthew was inspired," you might say, "so it was okay for him to use the Old Testament in this way." In other words, let's just sanitize the New Testament and simply attribute all instances of eastern, Hellenistic thinking to "inspiration."

Yet, we're only deceiving ourselves when we do that. Matthew's arguments were logical to his first century readers. In fact, the purpose of his writing was to convince the Jews that Jesus was the Messiah. He had to use arguments that would be convincing to *unbelievers*—people who didn't accept his writings as inspired.

Another example of eastern thinking in the New Testament is Paul's allegorical discussion of Sarah and Hagar in

Galatians 4:21-31. Or Paul's quotation to the Corinthians from Isaiah 28:11, which he applied to speaking in tongues: "In the Law it is written, 'By men of strange tongues and by the lips of strangers I will speak to this people, and even so they will not listen to me'" (1 Cor. 14:21). To western minds, the context of Isaiah 28:11 would hardly seem to be referring to speaking in tongues. Rather, it seems to be prophesying that Ephraim would be taken captive by the Assyrians. Finally, the entire Book of Hebrews, with its discussion of prophetic types and figures, is a classic example of eastern thinking.

The plain truth of the matter is that Matthew, Paul, and the other New Testament writers did not always think the way that we do. Nor did the Christians of the first and second centuries. The eastern, Hellenistic reasoning of the early Christian writers seems strange and foreign to us only because we have been reading the Scriptures through sanitized glasses.

And remember, it's a two-way street. If we find the reasoning of the early Christians strange, they would have found *our* reasoning strange as well. Unfortunately, the New Testament writings were addressed to them—not to us. They don't have to get into our twentieth-century, western mindset. We must get into their mindset.

Spiritual Truths from the Law

One of the first early Christian writings that I read was the Letter of Barnabas. Here I was treated to a detailed discussion of the spiritual truths that lay behind the Mosaic Law. For example, Barnabas wrote that God's prohibition to the Jews against eating pork had this spiritual message to Christians: "You are not to consort with the class of people who are like swine, inasmuch as they forget all about the

Lord while they are living in affluence, but remember Him when they are in want—just as a swine, so long as it is eating, ignores its master, but starts to squeal the moment it feels hungry, and then falls silent again when it is given food."[2]

When I first read this, I scoffed at this "absurd" spiritual lesson that Barnabas derived from the Jewish dietary law against pork. I stopped sneering, however, the next time I read Paul's words to the Corinthians about his right to receive material support: "I am not speaking these things according to human judgment, am I? Or does not the Law also say these things? For it is written in the Law of Moses, 'You shall not muzzle the ox while he is threshing.' God is not concerned about oxen, is He? Or is He speaking altogether for our sake? Yes, for our sake it was written" (1 Cor. 9:8-10).

I thought to myself, "Why did I never notice the significance of that passage before? Paul is pulling a spiritual principle out of the Mosaic Law that I would have never seen. And he says that passages like this in the Law were actually written for *our sake*. So why should I find it strange that Paul's disciples see similar principles in the Law?" Let's be honest. If we found this application of the Law about oxen in the Letter of Barnabas instead of in the writings of Paul, we would scoff at it, wouldn't we?

And please don't say that it was all right for Paul to do this only because he was inspired. Paul was presenting an argument in order to *persuade* his readers. He was trying to reason with them. A person doesn't reason with someone by throwing out an argument that makes no logical sense to them. No, Paul's argument made logical sense to his Corinthian readers. It was not dependent solely on inspiration.

Real People in a Real World

Please don't misunderstand me. I'm neither denying nor minimizing the inspiration of Scripture. What I am saying is that the New Testament writers were real people writing to other real people, all of whom lived in a real, historic world. It wasn't a sanitized, westernized, modern world. It was an ancient, eastern, Hellenistic world with its own thought patterns.

The other day, I saw a bumper sticker on a car that read, "If God seems far off, guess who has moved?" An equally valid question would be: If the Christianity that existed around A.D. 100 seems distant and strange to us, guess who's moved away from first century Christianity?

If it weren't for our reading it through sanitized filters, the New Testament would seem strange to us, too. Instead, we have so modernized, westernized, and sanitized the apostolic writers that we delude ourselves into thinking that John could step right from the first century into our western, twentieth century churches and feel quite at home. In contrast, we think that he would find the second century Church to be strange and foreign. Now who's kidding whom?

In short, the early Christian writings did more for me than to merely provide historic evidence of how the primitive Church understood Scripture. They also removed the blinders from my eyes so I could truly see the New Testament itself. They can do the same thing for you.

How to Read the Early Writings

However, before those writings can open your eyes, you will have to approach them with an open mind. As I was finally forced to do, you too will first have to temporarily set aside everything you believe. Just *listen* to what they have to say. Nobody is going to force you to *believe* anything they say. When you are through, you may choose to take back all of your own beliefs. I never did. But perhaps you will. Either way, you owe it to yourself to at least take an honest look at the historical evidence.

But be prepared for a journey back into time. Their culture is the same as that of the New Testament. The only difference is that nobody has "sanitized" their writings for you yet. Don't expect them to be living in a modern, western culture. Since their writings are not inspired, they reflect all of the scientific notions of their age—except where those notions expressly conflict with Scripture.*

One man has written a paper disparaging the early Christians because a few of the writers made reference to the phoenix bird. This was a bird that was supposed to have lived in the Arabian desert. According to legend, it lived for five or six hundred years, and then consumed itself in fire. However, it would arise anew from the ashes to begin another long life. This was not a fable invented by Christians. Rather, it was a legend that was widely believed in the ancient world. Since few people ever traveled into the Arabian desert, this legend was not easily refuted.

Naturally, the early Christians saw in the phoenix bird a representation of the resurrection from the dead. Why should we expect anything different? Again, these were real people living in a real world. Because they were Christians, it doesn't mean that they were somehow endowed with twentieth century zoological knowledge. Neither were the apostles. The only difference is that the Holy Spirit kept scientific errors out of the New Testament.

---

*Where there was conflict, the early Christians believed the Scriptures, rather than the scientific theories of their day.[3]

Also, as you read the early Christian writings, remember that you should not form any definite conclusions about what the whole Church believed until you have read *all* of their writings. You can't take just one writer's perspective as being the *whole* embodiment of early Christian beliefs. You have to look at what they all say.

But, again, that is no different than the New Testament writings. If a person read only one of the New Testament books and assumed that such was the entire message of apostolic Christianity, he would obviously be in error, wouldn't he? What if a person read nothing but the Book of James? Would he have a complete understanding of the New Testament teaching on salvation?

If my only interest were to entice you to read these historic writings, I would have omitted these last three chapters. I don't doubt that the things expressed in these chapters have probably made you feel a bit uneasy. In fact, you may be saying to yourself, "I don't need the early Christian writings. All I need is my Bible." But the truth is that you are presently using more than just your Bible. Let me explain.

15

The Real Issue

The issue is not the early Christian writings versus Scripture. Remember, the only reason we are looking at the early Christian works in the first place is to help us to correctly understand Scripture. There is no competition here between them and Scripture.

The real issue is *their* understanding of Scripture versus *our* understanding of Scripture. Let's go back to my illustration of the chair manufacturing contract. Are we going to try to *guess* what the contract means? Or are we going to look at the course of performance of Ezra Mast and James Butler, the original parties to the contract?

The early Christians were students of the Scriptures. In fact, it has been said that if all copies of the New Testament had been destroyed, it could essentially be restored merely from the quotations of the early Christian writers.[1] Their teachings are strongly supported by Scripture. After all, they, too, believed in the inspiration and inerrancy of Scripture.

In fact, virtually everything they taught can still be found today scattered among the various groups of conservative, Bible-believing Christians. Yet, no single group by itself holds to all of their teachings. There is basically no early Christian belief that some Protestant group hasn't taught simply on the basis of "Scripture alone."

For example, the Anabaptists held to most of the beliefs and practices of the early Christians. The Anabaptists grew out of the Reformation in sixteenth century Switzerland, and they emphasized living by the Sermon on the Mount. Because of their uncompromising walk with the Lord and their belief in separation of church and state, they were cruelly persecuted by the Catholic, Lutheran, and Reformed churches alike. Their descendants are still here today in the Mennonites, Amish, and Hutterites.*

Another Biblically-minded group whose teachings and practices are very similar to those of the early Church are the German Baptist Brethren. They began in the early 1700s out of a small fellowship of Christians in Germany who were committed to returning to primitive Christianity. They ended

---

*For further reading about the Anabaptists, I recommend *The Theology of Anabaptism*, by Robert Friedmann, published by Herald Press, 616 Walnut Ave., Scottdale, PA 15683, and *The Chronicle of the Hutterian Brethren*, published by Plough Publishing House, New Meadow Run Bruderhof, Farmington, PA 15437. The latter is also available from The Christian Community, Rt. 7, Box 247-A, Cookeville, TN 38501. Two good primary sources to go to are *The Complete Writings of Menno Simons* and *Anabaptism in Outline*, both of which are published by Herald Press.

up moving to America to escape persecution from the Lutheran and the Reformed state churches.*

So perhaps I shouldn't say that you are going to find the early Christian beliefs and practices to be radically different from yours. I don't even know what your beliefs are. All I know is that only about half of my beliefs matched those of the early Church. A few people will find that the early Christian beliefs are almost identical with their own. For example, I spent a Saturday afternoon with a man who was a real student of Scripture. He had never read the early Christian writings and really had little interest in them. Yet, through our discussion, I found that he held to nearly all of the same doctrines as did the early Church.

The Big Double Standard

Modern cults, such as Jehovah's Witnesses, generally teach that the Church became apostate almost immediately after the apostles died. "Therefore," they argue, "the historical record is of no value. Instead, we must interpret the Scriptures for ourselves without reference to what anyone believed in the past."

---

*This group should not be confused with the Plymouth Brethren, who are not related to them. One of the best books about the history of the German Baptist Brethren is *Counting the Cost,* by William G. Willoughby, published by The Brethren Press, 1451 Dundee Ave., Elgin, IL 60120. For additional information about the German Baptist Brethren, a person can write to their official publication, *The Vindicator*, 1876 Beamsville - Union City Rd., Union City, OH 45390. Two related groups who are similar in practice are the Old Brethren and the Dunkard Brethren. The Church of the Brethren is a more liberal branch of this same movement.

In contrast, orthodox Christians maintain that we cannot separate ourselves from historic Christianity. In our books against cults, we invariably boast that we are defending "historic Christianity." For example, in his book, *So What's The Difference?*, Fritz Ridenour writes, "The 'difference,' as far as this book is concerned, is between the historic Christian faith and some of the major religions and cults of the world."[2] In the book, *Handbook of Today's Religions,* Josh McDowell and Don Stewart give this definition of a cult: "A cult is a perversion, a distortion of biblical Christianity and/or rejection of the historic teachings of the Christian church."[3]

Yet, despite what we publicly say, many of our doctrines and practices *don't* match up to the historic teachings of the Church. And what is our response when that is brought to our attention? Do we then humbly change our beliefs to conform to those of the historic record? No, I'm afraid we don't. Instead, we suddenly change our tune and say that the early Christians were wrong. So after making much ado about the importance of "historic Christianity," we respond no differently than the cults when we come face to face with the real McCoy. Isn't that being a bit hypocritical?

In the end, the only boast that we can make is that our beliefs go back further than do those of the cults. But if our beliefs can't be traced all the way back to the beginning, of what value is that? On the other hand, if by "historic Christianity" we mean the doctrines that the Church developed over the centuries, then we should all be Roman Catholics or Eastern Orthodox.

Practically all Christians recognize the weight and value of the early Christian writings. For we instinctively quote from them *when they agree with us.* We offer their testimony as virtually incontrovertible evidence that the Church originally understood a particular doctrine the same way we do. Yet, when those writings don't agree with our positions, we immediately dismiss what they have to say as being of no value. What a double standard!

And God hates a double standard. "You shall not have in your bag differing weights, a large and a small. You shall not have in your house differing measures, a large and a small. You shall have a full and just weight; you shall have a full and just measure, that your days may be prolonged in the land which the Lord your God gives you. For everyone who does these things, everyone who acts unjustly is an abomination to the Lord your God" (Deut. 25:13-16). That passage is discussing double standards of weight and measure as to physical things. But is that principle any different as to spiritual things? If material dishonesty is wrong, is spiritual dishonesty any different?

One of the principal criticisms I have received over the past several years is that I "take the early Christian writings too seriously." Yet, I am only endeavoring to be spiritually honest. I strongly believe that none of us should use a double standard. We should either honestly accept the historical evidence of the early Christian writings, or we should quit quoting from them altogether. Either these people were orthodox Christians—or they were heretics. To quote them when they support our denomination's beliefs, and then call them heretics when they don't, is hypocritical.

"Fine! I'll do without them," you may be thinking. "All I need is my Bible." But you are *already* relying on the early Christians—probably without knowing it.

16

The Myth of
"Sola Scriptura"

Steve Scoggins (not his real name) is an earnest Christian and is well versed in Scripture. Several years ago, I was sharing with him some of these same things I have shared with you. After listening politely for about thirty minutes, he finally could keep quiet no longer. Shaking his head in disapproval, he blurted out "I'm sorry. That's all very interesting, but all I need is my Bible. I'm not going to accept anything if it's not in the Bible."

Noticing that his Bible was laying on the table next to him, I replied, "Steve, turn for a moment to the first book of the New Testament." He quickly complied. "Tell me," I continued, "who wrote that book?"

"Matthew did," he replied without hesitation.

"Now, tell me *why* you believe that Matthew wrote that book," I queried.

"Well, because it says so right at the top of the page," he answered with a grin.

"Steve," I explained, "none of the names that we use for the Bible books are part of the original manuscripts. For example, Paul didn't scribble '1 Corinthians' at the top of his letter to the Corinthians. No, all of the names of Bible books are names that humans have added as a means to quickly identify those books."

He didn't challenge me on this, so I continued, "So *now* tell me why you believe that Matthew wrote the first book of our New Testament."

Steve quickly began leafing through the Gospel of Matthew, quite certain he would find a place where the writer had identified himself. But he found nothing.

Finally, I halted him, "You can search carefully through the entire book, but you won't find any place where it says who the writer is. So let me tell you why you believe that Matthew wrote this book. You believe it because the early Christians say that Matthew wrote it!"

We then went through the same procedure with Mark. Then Luke. Then John. Then Acts. Each time the answer was the same. In none of those books does the writer identify himself. In each case, we have accepted without question the historic testimony of the early Christians.

"So," I asked him, "Do you *still* maintain that the writers of the four Gospels are Matthew, Mark, Luke, and John?"

"Sure!" he responded.

"Then you *do* accept things that aren't in the Bible, after all," I said with a smile.

And so does everyone else. If we really are going to accept *only Scripture,* then we need to take the Gospel names, "Matthew," "Mark," "Luke," and "John," out of our Bibles. We need to replace them with "First Gospel," "Second Gospel," "Third Gospel," and "Fourth Gospel."

Likewise, First John, Second John, and Third John should be listed in our Bibles simply as three anonymous letters.

What's more, if we are going to reject the testimony of the early Christians, we need to question our whole New Testament canon. Some Christians have the mistaken impression that at the close of the apostolic age the apostles handed the Church a bound collection of writings called the "New Testament," containing all of the books we have in our New Testament. But that's not what happened.

Rather, the early Christian congregations separately collected together the various letters and narrative accounts written by the apostles and disciples. The apostles never told the Church which writings to accept and which to reject. The early Christians had to decide for themselves which writings were genuinely from the apostles and which were not—which was no easy task. Our New Testament today is based upon the lists compiled by the early Christians. We heavily rely upon their testimony.

A Myth from the Start

"Sola Scriptura" ("Only Scripture") was the battle cry of the Reformation. Yet, that slogan was a myth from the very beginning. Although one of Martin Luther's noteworthy accomplishments was his translation of the Bible into German, he made certain that his readers would not have "sola Scriptura." He didn't want them to approach Scripture with a blank slate. So Luther inserted prefaces to each Bible book in his translation, and those prefaces steered the reader's attention away from parts of the Bible that didn't fit Luther's theology. For example, in his preface to the New Testament, Luther wrote:

> It would be right and proper that this book should appear without preface and without any other name

than that of its authors, and convey only its own name and its own language. But many wild interpretations and prefaces have driven the thought of Christians to a point where no one any longer knows what is Gospel or Law, Old Testament or New. Necessity demands, therefore, that it should have an announcement, or preface, by which the simple man can be brought back from the old notions to the right road, and be taught what he is to expect in this book, so that he may not seek laws and commandments where he ought to be seeking the Gospel and God's promises. . . .

If I had to do without one or the other—either the works or preaching of Christ—I would rather do without His works than His preaching; for the works do not help me, but His words give life, as He Himself says. Now John writes very little about the works of Christ, but very much about His preaching. But the other Evangelists write much of His works and little of His preaching. Therefore John's Gospel is the one, tender, true chief Gospel, far, far to be preferred to the other three and placed high above them. So, too, the Epistles of St. Paul and St. Peter far surpass the other three Gospels—Matthew, Mark and Luke.

In a word, St. John's Gospel and his first Epistle, St. Paul's Epistles, especially Romans, Galatians, and Ephesians, and St. Peter's first Epistle are the books that show you Christ and teach you all that it is necessary and good for you to know, even though you were never to see or hear any other book or doctrine. Therefore St. James' Epistle *is really an epistle of straw*, compared to them; for it has nothing of the nature of the Gospel about it.[1] (Italics mine.)

Luther claimed that the only reason he preferred the Gospel of John over the other three gospels was that it contained more of Jesus' preaching. But that isn't true. The Gospel of Matthew contains nearly *twice* as much of Jesus' preaching as does the Gospel of John. A person doesn't need to be very perceptive to see what Luther's real motive was. The Bible books Luther disparaged happen to be the very books that didn't support his theology.

Not only was Luther's translation not "sola Scriptura," but few of the other early Protestant Bibles were either. William Tyndale produced the first Protestant translation of the Bible into English. Yet, his translation is strewn with marginal notes that add interpretations and polemical remarks to the text of Scripture. For example, alongside the text of 1 Corinthians 14:2, which addresses speaking in tongues, Tyndale wrote, "To speak with tongues or with the spirit, is to speak that others understand not, as priests say their service. To speak with the mind is to speak that others understand, as when the preacher preacheth."[2] Alongside the text for Revelation 7, Tyndale explained, "Prophets, preachers and the prelates of the church are called angels. . . . The good angels here in this book are the true bishops and preachers, and the evil angels are the heretics and false preachers."[3] If Tyndale truly believed in "sola Scriptura," why couldn't he just let the Bible speak for itself?

The Geneva Bible, first published in 1560, was the work of English Protestant exiles who had taken refuge in Geneva, Switzerland. It was strewn throughout with marginal notes that added human interpretations to God's Word. One example is the interpretation it places alongside 1 Corinthians 14:1. Paul had written to the Corinthians about prophesying, saying, "Pursue love, yet desire earnestly spiritual *gifts,* but especially that you may prophesy" (1 Cor. 14:1). The Geneva Bible "illuminates" the word "prophesy" by commenting, "That is, to expound the word of God to the edification of the Church."[4] Alongside Revelation 9:1, which speaks of "a star from heaven which had fallen to the earth," the Geneva Bible interjects, "That is, the bishops and ministers who forsake the worship of God and who fall out of heaven and become angels of darkness."[5]

My point is not to discuss the merits of these various interpretations. Rather, I'm calling attention to the fact that the most popular early Protestant Bibles all added interpretative remarks alongside the text of Scripture.* "Sola Scriptura" was a myth from the start.

Just the Plain Bible?

Sadly to say, Protestants are no closer today to "sola Scriptura" than were their sixteenth century ancestors. Protestants today are purchasing interpretative study Bibles by the tens of thousands. By the term, "interpretative study Bibles," I'm not referring to Bibles that merely provide cross-references, maps, and a concordance, such as the *Personal Reference Bible, Nave's Study Bible, Discovery Bible,* and the *Thompson-Chain Reference Bible.* I have no problem with Bibles like these.

But most study Bibles go far beyond adding cross-references. They add human interpretations alongside Scripture. Some of these interpretative study Bibles are:

- *Ryrie Study Bible*
- *Scofield Reference Bible*
- *Dake's Annotated Reference Bible*

---

*One of the reasons the King James Version, first published in 1611, was such a spiritual landmark was that it was one of the first Protestant Bibles that was not embellished with running commentaries.

- *Salem Kirban Reference Bible*
- *NIV Study Bible*
- *Hebrew-Greek Key Study Bible*
- *Harper Study Bible*

What I find so objectionable about these study Bibles is that they print human interpretations and biases on the very same pages where God's Word appears. What incredible audacity! That gives man's words equal weight with God's. For example, in the *Hebrew-Greek Key Study Bible*, underneath Paul's discussion of the head covering in 1 Corinthians 11, the commentator writes:

> Paul is writing here to the Corinthian Christians who, living in Greece, customarily complied with Greek traditions: men had their heads uncovered and the women covered theirs, which, however, was contrary to the Jewish tradition. Even to this day, Jewish men cover their heads at worship, but not the women. The question which faced the Corinthians was what to do with the existing custom of their day. Paul's advice is to examine the symbolism of the custom. If it has nothing in it that is contrary to God's Word or order in creation, accept it. Do not allow contentions to arise regarding customs which symbolize something that is proper (vv. 13,16).

Oh, so Paul is merely giving "advice" to follow human, Greek customs! But did Paul say anything about Greek customs versus Jewish customs? No, rather he began his discussion by commending the Corinthians for holding "firmly to the traditions, just as *I delivered them* to you" (1 Cor. 11:2, italics mine). It was *Paul* who delivered the tradition of the head covering to the Corinthian Christians, not the pagan Greeks. The commentator is expressly contradicting what Paul said. Furthermore, there is nothing written in any of the historic, early Christian writings that would even remotely substantiate those comments. They are sheer human speculation. Yet, the commentator places them alongside Scripture, where they will influence the average Bible reader as much as Scripture.

In reality, study Bibles usually have the effect of giving man's words *more* weight than God's. I've sat in enough Bible studies to know that invariably people will take the commentator's opinions over the literal language of Scripture. I'm not singling out the *Hebrew-Greek Key Reference Bible* for criticism. Similar examples can be pulled from all of the interpretative study Bibles listed above. If "all we need is the Bible," as we publicly proclaim, why do we use such interpretative study Bibles?

Other Additions to Scripture

"But I don't use study Bibles," you may be saying. That's commendable. Yet, I would venture to say that you still don't use just the Bible alone. For instance, do you make use of Bible commentaries and Bible dictionaries? Do you read Christian literature? How about listening to sermons? If you make use of any of those things, then you are not using *just the Bible.*

If we truly believed that all we needed was just the Bible, then we wouldn't be using all of these other aids. A church that used nothing but the Bible would be a church that simply read from Scripture every Sunday, without any comment or sermon. I don't know of any church like that, do you? Nor am I advocating that our church meetings be like that.

Rather, the point is that we all use something in addition to Scripture. The only issue is *what* we should use. Will we rely on the historic witness of the early Christians to shed light on Scripture? Or will we rely on the modern witness of our pastors, Christian writers, and theologians. That's the issue.

What We Add to Scripture—And Take Away

Many churches today brag that they use "only the Bible." They claim that they don't add anything to it, nor take anything away from it. Typically, such churches have no use for the early Christian writings. Perhaps you belong to such a church. Of course, as we have already seen, such churches *do* use something besides Scripture, since they read Christian literature and listen to sermons. If nothing else, they add rationalizations of why we do not have to literally obey what's taught in Scripture.

What's more, usually members of those churches cannot even express what they believe without using language that is not in Scripture. I'm talking about such terms as *revival, legalism, Trinity, Incarnation, missionary, altar call,* and *born-again experience.* Even the term *Bible* is not a Scriptural term. I'm not saying that there is anything wrong with these terms. Some of them, like Trinity, we have borrowed from the early Church. The point I'm making is that we have all added so much to Scripture that most of us can't even talk about what we believe without using language that is not in Scripture.

If someone asked you what your church teaches, would you be able to simply hand them the New Testament and tell them to read it? If you believe that all we need is Scripture, you should be able to do that.

If our churches truly believe in Scripture alone, and truly use the Bible as their sole guide, why do they erase and rescind so many things in Scripture? "But, my church doesn't," you may reply. Well, let's see. We have been focusing on Paul's first letter to the Corinthians. Does your church believe and practice all of the things taught there? I'm speaking of things such as:

- Men praying with their heads uncovered and women praying with their heads covered (1 Cor. 11:3-16).
- Disassociating members who are immoral, covetous, idolaters, revilers, drunkards, or swindlers (1 Cor. 5:11).
- Not taking a brother to court (1 Cor. 6:1-7).
- Properly using spiritual gifts (1 Cor. 12).
- Women keeping silent in the church (1 Cor. 14:34).
- Greeting one another with a holy kiss (1 Cor. 16:20).

Does your church believe and practice the instructions Paul gave in his other letters? Such as:

- Appointing elders and deacons based upon the qualifications set forth by Paul in 1 Timothy 3.
- Women adorning themselves "with proper clothing, modestly and discreetly, not with braided hair and gold or pearls or costly garments" (1 Tim. 2:9).
- Men lifting up holy hands in prayer (1 Tim. 2:8).
- Maintaining a list of widows, sixty years or over, who meet the other qualifications given in 1 Tim. 5:9-10.

Does your church believe and practice the instructions Jesus gave to his followers? Such as:

- "Do not resist him who is evil; but whoever slaps you on your right cheek, turn to him the other also" (Matt. 5:39).
- "If anyone wants to sue you, and take your shirt, let him have your coat also" (Matt. 5:40).
- "Do not lay up for yourselves treasures upon earth" (Matt. 6:19).
- "Make no oath at all, either by heaven . . . or by the earth" (Matt. 5:34,35).
- "Everyone who divorces his wife, except for *the* cause of unchastity, makes her commit adultery; and whoever marries a divorced woman commits adultery" (Matt. 5:32).

I could go on, but these should be sufficient to illustrate my point. And my point is that, to my knowledge, no church today teaches and practices all of the things taught in Scripture. Yet, if our churches truly used just the Bible, leaving nothing out and adding nothing to it, then all churches would be obedient in all these matters. In contrast, the Church of the second century practiced all of the things listed above, along with all of the other New Testament teachings.

Yet, for the sake of argument, let's suppose for a moment that we did obey all of those teachings. Let's suppose that we truly do not add anything to Scripture. In other words, suppose that our Christianity was derived solely from what's written on the pages of Scripture. Even if that were the case, we would still need the early Christian writings in order to be obedient to Scripture. That's because there's a catch.

17

The Catch

That was a rather bold statement for me to make. So let me repeat it: If we don't *add* something to written Scripture, we are being disobedient to Scripture. Before you burn me at the stake, let me explain.

If your Bible is handy, turn to 2 Thessalonians 2:15: "So then, brethren, stand firm and hold to the traditions which you were taught, whether by word *of mouth* or by letter from us." Paul told the Thessalonian Christians *not* to go by written Scripture alone. They were to obey what the apostles taught, whether orally or by letter.

Let me ask you: Do you obey what the apostles taught "by word of mouth"? After all, aren't we under the same commandments that they were? If the Thessalonians were obligated to be obedient to what Paul taught orally, are we any less obligated?

In his same letter to the Thessalonians, Paul reiterated the need to be obedient to apostolic tradition: "Now we command you, brethren, in the name of our Lord Jesus Christ, that you keep aloof from every brother who leads an unruly life and not according to the tradition which you received from us" (2 Thess. 3:6). And as we noticed in 1 Corinthians 11:2, Paul praised the Corinthians for holding "firmly to the traditions, just as I delivered them to you."

I was raised to believe that *all* tradition is bad. The Bible passage that always popped into my mind when I heard the word "tradition" was Jesus' words to the Pharisees, "You invalidate the word of God for the sake of your tradition" (Matt. 15:6). Yet, as we have seen, that is only *one* of the New Testament passages about tradition. There is good tradition, and there is bad tradition. There is apostolic tradition, and there is human tradition. Apostolic tradition confirms what is written in Scripture. Human tradition makes Scripture invalid.

Let's go back to our discussion about the head covering. As I have said, this is not a book about head veiling. Yet, the subject nicely illustrates my point. Think about the tradition you have received concerning the head covering. Does it prompt you to obey what Scripture teaches on the subject? Or does it "invalidate the word of God"? Apostolic tradition—what was handed down orally by the apostles—never invalidates Scripture.

But how do we know what the apostles taught orally? Well, how would the next generation of Thessalonian Christians have known what Paul taught orally? They would have asked the first generation, wouldn't they? And how would the third generation have known? Right. They would have asked the second generation.

So where does that leave us—scores of generations later? If we use common sense, it leaves us in about the same situation as the third or fourth generation of Christians. That's because we have a historical record of the beliefs and practices of those early generations of Christians. In fact, the apostolic tradition is better attested to than most other historical facts.

What Is "Apostolic Tradition?"

"Are you saying that unless a person reads the early Christian writings, he cannot even be saved or be a real Christian?" you may be wondering. No, I'm not saying that at all. If a person found the New Testament in the desert and never read anything but it, he would have everything necessary to know the way of salvation and to have a close, obedient relationship with God. In fact, if that's *all* he had, he would be far better off than most of us. That's because he wouldn't have all of our human traditions. And he wouldn't have any ready-made reasons for ignoring Scripture.

Let me reassure you: the oral teachings or tradition of the apostles do not contain any theological doctrines that do not have a basis in Scripture. And they do not contain any moral teachings that are not an application of what is already in Scripture. So what's left? Plenty.

The primary value and function of apostolic tradition was to clarify and explain things that were written in Scripture. *We* find it necessary to expound and amplify the Scriptures, don't we? Do you think the apostles found any less of a need? The apostles didn't abandon the Church to a chaos of varied theological opinions, as we have today. They didn't leave it up to the first century Christians to guess how various moral teachings should be applied. No, the early Church was *one* body because it had apostolic tradition alongside Scripture. It didn't have to guess what Scripture meant; it had the explanations given by the apostles.

Apostolic tradition supplied them with another key thing—the proper method of practicing the "ordinances." By that term, I mean things such as the mode of baptism. The nature of church meetings. The day of the week to meet together for worship. The method of having communion. The frequency of communion. And the nature and frequency of love feasts. The Bible gives us some *clues* on these things. But it does not give us explicit instructions.

Actually the real issue isn't—"the Bible alone" versus "the Bible plus tradition." Rather, the issue is—"the Bible plus apostolic tradition" versus "the Bible plus man-made tradition." That's because every Christian subscribes to some type of tradition. It's either apostolic tradition or its man-made tradition. My dictionary defines tradition as "the handing down orally of beliefs, customs, etc. from generation to generation."[1] So every sermon you have ever heard is a form of tradition. Every piece of Christian literature you have ever read is extra-Biblical tradition.

If your church has a position on how to harmonize Romans with James, that's tradition. If it has explanations to harmonize other seemingly contradictory Bible passages, that's tradition. If your church advocates a particular mode of baptism—or doesn't advocate a mode—that's tradition. Whether your church holds communion every week, every month, every quarter, or only once a year, it has *some* tradition about communion. Even the nature and frequency of your church meetings are a tradition.

There really is no way to get around tradition. That being the case, isn't it simply common sense to try to determine what the traditions of the apostles were and to follow them? The early Christians specifically claimed that their teachings, practices, and ordinances had all been handed down to them by the apostles. They were in a position to make that claim. We aren't.

Interestingly, virtually all of our church splits over the past 500 years have been over matters that were covered by apostolic tradition. So isn't the sensible thing to do, the humble thing to do, to look at the historic record to uncover the authentic apostolic tradition, and then to follow it? Why is that suggestion such a distasteful thing to most of us? Is it perhaps because of our pride?

Church Customs

There is a final group of matters covered by apostolic tradition that I will call "church customs." These are practices of the early Church that have no direct reference to Scripture. I'm speaking of things such as: Their annual commemoration of the day of Christ's resurrection. Their painting or carving the figure of the cross on homes and places of worship. Their tracing the sign of the cross on the forehead of a newly baptized person. Their use of the symbol of the *ichthys* or fish in Christian art. Their fasting on Wednesdays and Fridays. Their praying daily at 9:00, 12:00, and 3:00, in addition to unscheduled prayer times.

I am not insisting that Christians follow these practices that have no direct reference in Scripture. Yet, I am convinced that most of these things—but probably not all of them—were indeed traditions handed down by the apostles. For example, there is solid historic testimony that the annual commemoration of Christ's resurrection was a tradition handed down from the apostles.[2] The early Christians called it *Pascha* (Passover); English-speaking Christians today usually call it Easter. Unfortunately, many of our present-day Easter customs—and even the name "Easter"—are of pagan origin.

As I said, I doubt that every single custom of the second century Church was handed down by the apostles. I would guess that a few of their customs were man-made. The problem is that we have no way of separating the human tradition from the apostolic. So, personally, I think the wisest course is to observe all of their customs—unless there's a Scriptural reason not to. That's because most of their customs are probably part of the authentic apostolic tradition that we are all commanded to follow (2 Thess. 2:15). Not only that, but our following such customs would bring us closer to both the historic, ancient Church and to each other.

After all, most Christians today follow *some* of these traditions. For example, most Christians throughout the world celebrate *Pascha* or Easter. Most of us use representations of the cross on buildings or in art. And many of us use the *ichthys* or fish symbol. Yet, we evangelical Protestants are very inconsistent about this. We follow some early Christian customs, such as Easter and the fish symbol, but we ignore others, such as tracing the sign of the cross on the forehead. There is no logical pattern as to which traditions we have kept and which ones we have discarded.

What's even more ludicrous is that, after discarding many of the ancient Christian customs, we have added a host of our own traditions that are neither found in Scripture nor in the early Christian writings. Christmas would be the paradigm example of this. Not only was it unknown to the early Church, but also most Christmas customs are actually of pagan origin. For some reason, Protestants seem to be more comfortable with pagan customs than with early Christian customs.

So, try as we may, we never get back to "just the Bible," because the written Word tells us to be obedient to the oral tradition. But there's still another catch.

18

The Other Catch

The second catch is that nearly all of us read Scripture through a translation. And, to one degree or another, all translations are interpretations. And they aren't *unbiased* interpretations.

Bible translators are almost inevitably the products of seminary or university training. Even those who are more open minded and intellectually honest still don't start out with blank slates. They normally still have some sort of bias, whether it is liberal or evangelical, Catholic or Protestant. Many of them read their own theology into Scripture, and it affects their translations. Often a translator will have such strong preconceptions that he will even alter what the Biblical text says in order to make it fit his preconceptions.

Scripture Tampering

The classic example of such biased translating is the *New World Translation* published by Jehovah's Witnesses. In numerous places, this translation adds words to the Biblical text to support Witness theology. To illustrate, the *New World Translation* renders Colossians 1:16, which speaks about Jesus, as follows: "By means of him all [other] things were created in the heavens and upon the earth, the things visible and the things invisible. . . . All [other] things have been created through him and for him." In order to support their theology that Jesus is part of creation, those translators found it necessary to add the word "other" to the text. At least they were "honest" enough to place their added word in brackets.

Unfortunately, Jehovah's Witnesses are not the only ones who have purposefully altered Scripture in order to support their views. Evangelicals are no less guilty than they are.* For example, Martin Luther did not hesitate to add words to Scripture in order to bolster his theology. The most famous example is his adding the word "alone" to Romans 3:28, making it say: "Therefore, we conclude that a man is justified by faith *alone,* apart from the works of the law." When Luther's hand was called on this, his arrogant reply was: "If your papist makes much useless fuss about the word alone, tell him at once, 'Doctor Martin Luther will have it so,' and says, 'Papist and donkey are one and the same thing.'"[1]

However, the most blatant example of evangelical tampering with Scripture is perhaps *The Living Bible.* It presently outsells all Bible translations except the *New International Version*, the King James Version, and the *New King James Version.*[2] It purports to be a paraphrased translation that expresses "as exactly as possible what the writers of the Scriptures meant."[3] Yet, it alters so many

---

*I'm not equating the doctrinal purposes of evangelical tampering with the doctrinal errors of Jehovah's Witnesses. I'm only equating the tendency of both groups to tamper with Scripture.

things in the Bible text that it should be marketed as a commentary, not a Bible translation. Let me illustrate:

Paul wrote to the Romans: "Because by the works of the Law no flesh will be justified in His sight; for through the Law *comes* the knowledge of sin. But now apart from the Law *the* righteousness of God has been manifested, being witnessed by the Law and the Prophets" (Rom. 3:20,21). Notice how *The Living Bible* grossly alters the text: "Now do you see it? No one can ever be made right in God's sight by doing what the law commands. For the more we know of God's laws, the clearer it becomes that we aren't obeying them; his laws serve only to make us see that we are sinners. But now God has shown us a different way to heaven—not by 'being good enough' and trying to keep his laws, but by a new way (though not new, really, for the Scriptures told about it long ago)."

That's expressing "as exactly as possible" what Paul meant to say? Why, the translator has literally doubled the size of the text by all of his human additions. In no shape or form is that a translation or even a paraphrase of what Paul said. It's an interpretation—a commentary. Yet, *The Living Bible* is used and endorsed by thousands of evangelical pastors. What a double standard we have. We castigate Jehovah's Witnesses for tampering with God's Word—and rightly so—yet we smile with approval when one of *our* people does the same thing to a far greater degree.

Presently, the best-selling Bible in America is the *New International Version*.[4] No doubt it has become the most popular translation because its translators did such an outstanding job of rendering the Scriptures into flowing, readable English. Unfortunately, its translators couldn't resist tampering with God's Word, either. One example is their rendition of Romans 2:28: "A man is not a Jew if he is only one outwardly, nor is circumcision merely outward and physical." Neither the word "only" nor the word "merely" are in the Greek text. The addition of those words can change Paul's meaning quite a bit. The rendering of the New International Version implies that a person must first be a Jew outwardly before he can be one inwardly. But that is not what Paul said.[5]

Even worse is the *New International Version's* marginal rendition given in its footnote to the passage we have been studying in 1 Corinthians. This marginal rendition reads: "Every man who prays or prophesies with long hair dishonors his head. And every woman who prays or prophesies with no covering [of hair] on her head dishonors her head—she is just like one of the 'shorn women.' If a woman has no covering, let her be for now with short hair, but since it is a disgrace for a woman to have her hair shorn or shaved, she should grow it again. A man ought not to have long hair" (1 Cor. 11:4-7). That's almost as bad as *The Living Bible.* That rendition is in no way an alternate translation of the Greek text. It's nothing more than a fanciful interpretation or a commentary.

The reason I am mentioning these examples is to illustrate that human biases sometimes alter the very words that appear on the pages of our Bibles. Even if we never read another piece of literature, we would still be receiving at least some human tradition through the pages of our Bibles.

We can minimize those biases by using a literal translation, such as the *New American Standard* or the King James Version. Yet even those translations have a degree of interpretation in them. In fact, even if you were fluent in *koine* Greek and could read the Greek text yourself, you would still be adding a good bit of your own translational interpretations to the text of Scripture. There's no way around it. Let me explain.

First of all, most words in Greek have more than one meaning, just as most English words do. So the translator has to make an interpretation in selecting which definition to apply to any given verse.

Secondly, in the most ancient texts we have of the New Testament, every letter of every word is capitalized. The effect is the same as if the texts were written in all small, or lower case, letters. When someone translates these texts into English, he must decide which words to capitalize. Whether or not a word is capitalized can significantly affect its meaning. For example, the Greek word *pneuma* (spirit) appears 27 times in Paul's letter to the Romans. For each occurrence, the translator must interpret whether Paul is speaking about the Holy Spirit or *our* spirit.

Spirit or spirit?

Notice how the *New American Standard* translates the passage from Romans 8:4-6: "In order that the requirement of the Law might be fulfilled in us, who do not walk according to the flesh, but according to the Spirit. For those who are according to the flesh set their minds on the things of the flesh, but those who are according to the Spirit, the things of the Spirit. For the mind set on the flesh is death, but the mind set on the Spirit is life and peace." As you noticed, the *New American Standard* translators interpreted Paul to be contrasting the flesh with the Holy Spirit. And they may be correct.

At the same time, Paul may have been talking about our human spirit, contrasting our *flesh* to our *spirit*. If that's what Paul meant, then the message of Romans is considerably different than what the Reformers preached. One of Luther's classic texts was Romans 7:18: "For I know that nothing good dwells in me, that is, in my flesh." Is Paul saying that nothing good dwells in a human being (as Luther interpreted it)? Or, is he saying that nothing good dwells in our *flesh* (as contrasted with our spirit)?[6] This is not merely some technical triviality. As I said, some of the basic doctrines of the Reformation turn on whether some of these verses are saying Spirit or spirit.

The word "spirit" can even take on a third meaning: "But now we have been released from the Law, having died to that by which we were bound, so that we serve in newness of the Spirit and not in oldness of the letter" (Rom. 7:6). That translation from the *New American Standard* interprets Paul to be contrasting the 'oldness of the letter' with the newness of the Holy Spirit. But perhaps Paul was contrasting the oldness of the literal *letter* of the Law with the newness of the *spirit* of the Law. Quite a different meaning. Yet, either rendition is linguistically correct.

The point here is not to detour into a discussion of theology. Rather, I'm illustrating the fallacy of our saying that we rely on "the Bible alone." We have no choice but to add something to the Bible. If nothing else, we must add an interpretation of how to translate the Greek.

The issue of capitalization is not the only interpretive problem in translating ancient Greek. The Greek of the New Testament also had no commas or quotation marks. So the translator has to interpret where to place commas and quotation marks. I know only too well as an attorney how the placement of a comma can significantly change the meaning of a sentence.

I'm not bringing up all of these things in order to undermine your confidence in the Scriptures. Rather, I want your confidence to be based on truth and sound reasoning—not on blindness. Our Bible translations need to read the way the apostles would have intended them to read.

An Early Church Translation?

Once again, we find ourselves back at a familiar juncture in the road: Should we rely upon the historic understandings of the early Christians when we translate the New Testament? Or should we rely upon our own understandings? How can we even evaluate how scriptural or unscriptural the early Christian teachings were until we translate Scripture the way they were understanding it?

There have been over fifty different translations made of the New Testament into English. Yet, not one of these translations has attempted to translate the Greek the way the early Christians understood it. But what better place is there to go for historic evidence of how the New Testament terms were used and understood by the people of that time period?

Do we really think we understand the informal Greek of the New Testament better than the second century Christians did? Remember, for most of them, *koine* Greek was their everyday language. Wouldn't common sense dictate that, when the Greek text can be translated in more than one way (such as Spirit vs. spirit), we should lean heavily on *their* understandings of what the Bible writers were saying, rather than our own? After all, some of them had the opportunity to ask Paul for clarification.

In short, there is simply no way to take "just the Bible" as our sole source of authority. Out of sheer necessity, we all add tradition and translational interpretation to the bare letter of Scripture. Doesn't common sense dictate that we should go to the historic record for our tradition and translations? Still, you may have some sincere questions about these early Christian writings before taking the plunge. Let's look at some of the questions I'm asked most frequently.

19

Sincere Questions About The Early Church Writings

Since writing *Will The Real Heretics Please Stand Up* several years ago, I have received hundreds of letters from persons with questions about the early Church. Many have asked sincere questions about the value and reliability of the early Christian writings. Let's take a look at some of these questions.

Won't the Holy Spirit Guide Us to All Truth?

It seems pretty hard to get Christians to agree on much of anything nowadays. Still, over the past couple of years, five different sincere Christians have written me, none of whom knew the others. But they were in perfect agreement on one point: We don't need the early Christian writings to correctly understand Scripture. Rather, they said, "the Holy Spirit will guide us to all truth" (John 16:13).

It crossed my mind to put all five of those persons in touch with each other, since they were united on the issue of how Christians can find truth. Yet, somehow I don't think they would have appreciated my doing so. For, you see, they all had a different opinion about what was true. Each was sure the Holy Spirit had guided him to "all truth," but each had arrived at a different "truth."

If all Christians were following the Holy Spirit's guidance to *all* truth, then all Christians would believe and teach the same things, wouldn't they? Yet, we are divided into over 22,000 different denominations and sects—all with differing beliefs.[1] So where have we gone wrong?

First of all, the Scriptures do not say that the Holy Spirit will give *direct revelation* of all truth to every Christian. The Holy Spirit guides us to truth through the written pages of Scripture and through the historic witness of the oral apostolic tradition. Just because we have the Holy Spirit's guidance doesn't mean that we don't need to look at the historic "course of performance" of the early Church. Would we claim that we don't need the Bible because we have the Holy Spirit's guidance?

It's for good reason that God doesn't normally give direct revelation of "all truth" to each one of us. Christ doesn't want a cluster of Lone Rangers out here who have no need of each other. He wants a Church. He wants one Body, a Body that is dependent not only on each other, but on the Church of the preceding centuries, as well. "Rugged individualism" might be what fueled America's rise to power, but it's not what fuels the Church. If the Holy Spirit directly revealed all necessary truth to the apostles, and they revealed it to the Church, why should we expect the Spirit to directly reveal those same truths all over again to each one of us? The early Christians were content to receive the

Christian truths "second hand" through the apostles and the apostolic Church. Why aren't we?

Interestingly, the early Christians understood John 16:12,13 to apply only to the apostles, at least as to direct revelation from God.* They truly believed that all spiritual truth had been revealed to the apostles. That's why they insisted that the Church must hold on to everything handed down by the apostles. They never claimed any special revelation beyond the apostles. In contrast, it was the heretics—the gnostics and the Montanists—who were not content merely to receive what had been delivered to the Church. Instead, they claimed special direct doctrinal revelation from the Holy Spirit.[2]

---

*The context of Jesus' words in John 16:13 would support the early Church's understanding of this passage. First of all, let's look at the setting. The scene was right after Jesus and the apostles had eaten the Last Supper. Judas Iscariot had already left. Jesus was giving parting words of counsel to His eleven faithful apostles. In the course of this counsel, He told them, "I have many more things to say to you, but you cannot bear *them* now. But when He, the Spirit of truth, comes, He will guide you into all the truth; for He will not speak on His own initiative, but whatever He hears, He will speak; and He will disclose to you what is to come" (John 16:12,13).

Notice that those words were *not* spoken to the crowds, or even to the seventy disciples Jesus sent out. They were spoken only to the eleven apostles. And not everything Jesus said to His apostles applies to all Christians, at least not to the same degree. In fact, this passage is actually a reiteration of what He had told the apostles moments before: "But the Helper, the Holy Spirit, whom the Father will send in My name, He will teach you all things, and bring to your remembrance all that I said to you" (John 14:26).

Would anyone argue that this parallel passage applies to all Christians? Jesus said the Spirit would 'bring to remembrance all of the things He had said to them.' Does anyone claim today that the Holy Spirit has brought to their memory all of the things Jesus said to His apostles?

I think that a lot of the ambiguity in Scripture was put there *purposefully* by God. He didn't want independent-minded persons to be able to take just Scripture by itself and then think they could separate themselves from the Church that his Son established.

Our Protestant attitude towards apostolic tradition sometimes resembles that of the gnostics. As Irenaeus said about them, "When we refer them to that tradition which originates from the apostles, and which is preserved by means of the successions of elders in the churches, they object to tradition, saying that they themselves are wiser, not merely than the elders, but even than the apostles, because they have discovered the unadulterated truth."[3]

Remember, if the Holy Spirit guides *us* to all truth, then He also guided the Christians of the second and third centuries to all truth as well. Our truth should be the same as theirs. If it's not, one of us has not been following the Holy Spirit's guidance.

Relying upon the historic "course of performance" of the early Church does not diminish the work of the Holy Spirit one iota. I believe that it was the Holy Spirit's guidance that led me to the witness of the early Church in the first place. I believe the Spirit would lead all Christians back to that witness if only we could put aside our prejudices and preconceptions. And it is only by the anointing of the Spirit that we can walk down that same pilgrim road that the early Christians followed.

Were the Early Christian Writings Accurately Preserved?

The early Christian writings are a valuable historic source only if the manuscripts we have of their writings are authentic. So let me say this, next to Scripture itself, few ancient writings are better attested to than the early Christian writings of the first and second centuries.

For example, the oldest Greek manuscript we have of the entire New Testament is the Codex Sinaiticus. It dates back to the fourth century (A.D.300-399). That codex also contains the Epistle of Barnabas and a portion of the Shepherd of Hermas, both of which are early Christian writings. In fact, some papyri manuscripts that date back to around the year 290 also contain a sizable portion of the Shepherd of Hermas.

Another one of our oldest manuscripts of the New Testament is the Codex Alexandrinus. It dates back to the fifth century (A.D. 400-499). In addition to our New Testament, it also contains the letter to the Corinthians written by Clement of Rome, as well as the text of an early Christian sermon, generally known as Second Clement. Although most of our manuscripts of early Christian writings do not date back that far, I know of no scholar—Catholic, Protestant, or agnostic—who questions the authenticity of these works. It's true that for some of the works all we have is one manuscript. Yet, the teachings of those works harmonize nicely with the teachings of the other works that have better manuscript support.

"But how do we know that the Roman Catholic Church didn't alter these writings to make them fit Catholic theology?" people often ask me. For one thing, the Roman Catholic Church didn't have control over most of these manuscripts. These manuscripts have been sheltered in a variety of geographical places—from western Europe to Africa, from the Mideast to Russia. Several of the works have been preserved in a variety of languages: Greek, Latin, Syriac, Armenian, Coptic, Arabic, Ethiopic, Georgian, and

Slavonian. No single church or person had control over these documents to be able to falsify them.

Secondly, the Roman Catholic Church had no particular need to falsify these writings, for it does not view most of the pre-Nicene writers as church fathers. The "great fathers" of the Roman Catholic Church include none of the pre-Nicene writers. Instead, they are Augustine, Ambrose, Jerome, Gregory the Great, Athanasius, Basil, Gregory of Nazianzus, and John Chrysostom—all of whom lived during or after the fourth century.[4]

So, rather than falsifying the early Christian writings, to a large degree the post-Nicene Church simply ignored them. Oh, a few fake writings did circulate, such as a number of spurious letters attributed to Ignatius. Yet, these forgeries have all been pretty well exposed. And no scholars today are claiming that any of these forgeries are genuine.

Actually, the very content of the writings themselves testifies convincingly that the Roman Catholic Church has not doctored up these works. That's because these writings don't support many of the key teachings of today's Catholic Church. In fact, they don't completely fit *any* denomination. The early Christians were neither Catholic nor Protestant, in the modern sense of the words. They are in a class by themselves. Their writings breathe a pristine, ancient quality that is not seen in later writings. They contradict some of the major teachings of both the Reformers and the Roman Catholic Church.

Furthermore, in the West, for nearly a thousand years, a substantial portion of these writings were actually forgotten. They didn't come back into general circulation until *after* the Reformation. By then, the tenets of the Reformation were set in stone, and nobody was willing to change them. So, once again, to a large degree, the Western Church simply ignored these invaluable writings.

Weren't the Early Christians
Heavily Influenced by Greek Philosophy?

One of the most frequently used means of disparaging the early Christians is to accuse them of having taken their teachings from Greek philosophy. It's also one of the most irresponsible. Usually it's made by someone who has read neither the early Christian works nor those of the Greek philosophers. The accuser is quite unable to show you *where* in the writings of the Greek philosophers they find the same teachings as those of the early Church.

Sometimes the persons who make this accusation also claim that Jesus, Paul, and John also took their teachings from Greek philosophers, or from the Qumran community.[5] Some of them also assert that Moses took the Ten Commandments from the Code of Hammurabi and that Daniel took his teachings from the Persian religious teacher, Zoroaster. Actually, there is no more evidence that the early Church took its teachings from Greek philosophy than there is for those other claims.

Not only that, the general attitude of the early church towards philosophy was one of antagonism. Tertullian called philosophers the "patriarchs of heretics."[6] Hippolytus included the philosophers among the false teachers in his comprehensive work, *The Refutation of All Heresies.**

---

*Justin Martyr and Clement of Alexandria were notable exceptions to the general antipathy of the early Church towards the Greek philosophers. Justin and Clement both believed that some Greek philosophy reflected seeds of truth that God had planted with the Gentiles to help show them the way to Christianity. However, neither Justin nor Clement based their Christian beliefs upon Greek philosophy. They taught the same things as did those other early Christians who were antagonistic towards philosophy.

Finally, it should be remembered that many early Christian writings were apologies, written to explain Christianity to non-believers. The apologists skillfully used quotations from the philosophers for the purpose of demonstrating the reasonableness of Christianity to the educated Romans. For example, in his *First Apology,* Justin pointed out to his Roman readers various resemblances between the teachings of Christianity and the tenets of various philosophers. But in his apologetic work written to the Jews, entitled *Dialogue with Trypho, A Jew,* Justin quoted heavily from Moses and the Old Testament prophets. In other words, he used the arguments that would have the most weight with his audience.

Paul used the very same approach when witnessing to the court of the Areopagus in Athens. Noticing an altar dedicated to "an unknown God," he told the council: "For while I was passing through and examining the objects of your worship, I also found an altar with this inscription, 'To an Unknown God.' What therefore you worship in ignorance, this I proclaim to you. . . . for in Him we live and move and exist, as even some of your own poets have said, 'For we also are His offspring'" (Acts 17:23,28). It would be rather absurd, wouldn't it, to claim that Paul derived his beliefs from the Greek poets, simply because he quoted from one of them when preaching to the Greeks. Is the accusation against the early Christians any less absurd?

Didn't They Use Strange Hermeneutical Principles?

Another common accusation made against the early Christians is that their hermeneutics were so weird that their writings are of no use to anyone. By hermeneutics, I mean their methods of Bible interpretation. The accusation against the early Christians is based partly on the fact that they often used eastern, Hellenistic reasoning that is very foreign to us. But as we've seen, the New Testament writers used the very same type of reasoning.

Furthermore, one of the distinguishing features of the second century Christians is their ultra-*literal* interpretation of the New Testament. You can point to any commandment or moral teaching in the New Testament, and I can almost guarantee you that the early Church took it very literally and very seriously. Take for example our discussion about the prayer covering. It's the twentieth century Church that has given a fanciful interpretation to the passage in 1 Corinthians 11, not the second century Church. Their understanding is very literal.

Actually, early Christian New Testament hermeneutics closely follow the common sense principles we have discussed:

1. They began with a blank slate. There had been no church councils or theological battles to influence them. There were no seminaries or denominations. At the beginning of the second century, there was little Christian literature, except for the Scriptures. Their minds were blank slates that the apostles and their disciples could write on.

2. Their understanding of Christianity and the New Testament began with Jesus Christ and His teachings. They always understood Paul and the other apostles in the context of Jesus' teachings, not vice versa.

3. Almost without exception, they took every New Testament passage very literally—and very seriously.

4. Their beliefs nearly always took into account the *whole* of what the New Testament teaches on any subject.

5. They leaned heavily on the "course of performance" of the apostles and the generation of Christians who were taught directly by the apostles. Their whole credo was to hold on to the things handed down by the apostles and not to change them.

6. Finally, their understanding of parts of the New Testament do not render other parts of the New Testament void or unreasonable. As a result, their theology doesn't have nearly as many "problem verses" to explain away as does Reformation and modern theology.

So it's not *their* hermeneutics that are "weird"; it's often *our* systems of interpretation that are strange by common sense standards.

Do They Really Clarify Scripture?

One person has raised the question, "Aren't the early Christian writings just as ambiguous as Scripture? Rather than helping us to understand Scripture, don't they just give us one more thing to interpret?"

It's true that the early Christian writings suffer from the same limitations of human language as do the Scriptures. Our modern Christian books have those limitations as well. Yet, we don't hesitate to turn to modern books to help us understand Scripture, do we? Likewise, although the early Christian writings contain ambiguities, that doesn't prevent them from shedding important light on the Scriptures.

A good example is Tertullian's essay on the head covering that I previously cited. Not everything that Tertullian says in that essay is perfectly clear. Yet, I don't think anyone could possibly read his essay and wonder whether the head covering was a cloth veil or simply long hair. That part is absolutely clear. And that's all we were after.

There is a saying, "When you're up to your neck in alligators, it's easy to forget that the reason you were in the swamp in the first place was to drain it." Remember, the main reason we were looking at the early Christian writings in the first place was to determine the historic "course of performance" of the New Testament church.* And in this they do an admirable job. But these writings are not some kind of "second canon" in their own right that we have to thoroughly understand the way we do Scripture. It's not essential that we clarify every ambiguity in them.

Of course, the early Christian works don't clarify every verse in the New Testament. But they do reveal the "course of performance" of the first few generations of Christians in the key doctrinal areas, in their ordinances, and in their application of Biblical commands. They also reveal what the primitive church considered to be the essential doctrines of Christianity. Through the centuries, many Christians have proclaimed the motto: "In necessary things, unity; in doubtful things, liberty; in all things, charity."[7] I think we would probably all agree with this credo. But what are the "necessary things" of the Christian faith? What are the "doubtful things"? Who decides?

Again, this is where the early Christians give us invaluable insight. If the faith was "once for all handed down to the saints," shouldn't we let the disciples of the apostles tell us what things were considered "necessary" and what things were considered "doubtful"? If certain doctrines weren't clear to the disciples of the apostles, how can they be any more clear to us? Or, are we going to claim that we have special revelation that they didn't have?

---

*These writings are also our primary source of knowledge about oral apostolic tradition.

This is why I steadfastly maintain that we Bible-believing Christians could all be one if we would simply humble ourselves and accept the witness of what historic Christianity really was. It would not mean that we would have uniformity on every belief. Rather, it would mean that we would have uniformity on the essential doctrines and that we would not split over the others because we would recognize them for being what they are: "doubtful" or peripheral.

Of course, the testimony of the early Christians is pivotal on these matters only if they were faithfully preserving the faith delivered to them by the apostles. How can we be reasonably sure that they were?

20

Did the Church
Remain Faithful?

Did the first few generations of Christians after the apostles faithfully preserve "the faith that was once for all handed down to them?" Or did Christianity collapse right after the apostles died, as sects like Jehovah's Witnesses claim? Let's examine all the evidence to see.*

If Christian beliefs and practices changed between the first and second centuries, then the change had to have come about in one of two ways. First, the change could have come about *deliberately*. The second and third generations of

---

*I addressed this issue in chapters 11 and 12 of my book, *Will The Real Heretics Please Stand Up*. Rather than repeating all of the information I shared in those chapters, I refer the reader to that book, if he has not already read it. However, I am summarizing the basic arguments presented there.

Christians may have purposefully changed what had been handed down to them. However, they specifically say over and over again in their writings that what they are defending is what the apostles themselves taught. They also believed, as we have said, that there was no further special revelation after the apostles.[1]

"Sure, but they could still be *lying,*" you might say. In other words, these writers may have been liars—apostates—who were purposely misrepresenting Christ and the apostles. Yet, when we read of their godly lives and their willingness to give up all for Christ, I don't think any of us really want to say that. What's more, thousands of them—including quite a few of the writers—suffered imprisonment in dark, foul dungeons; endured excruciating tortures; and suffered horrible deaths rather than to deny Christ. Is that something deliberate liars would do? How many people would suffer torture and death for something they knew was a lie? So the first method of change—deliberate apostasy—is highly unlikely.

However, change could still have come about a second way: accidentally. In other words, the Christians of the second century may have been diligently trying to teach and practice what was handed down to them, but they somehow misunderstood what the apostles had taught.

But how could that be? Some of the early Christian writers, such as Polycarp and Clement of Rome, received the gospel directly from the apostles. How could they possibly have misunderstood them? If *they* did, what hope is there for us? Other early Christian writers, such as Irenaeus, received the gospel from those who had secured it directly from the apostles.

"Well, then," you might say, "perhaps change came about slowly, almost imperceptibly. But after awhile, by the accumulation of these small changes, the Church had drifted

pretty far from the original gospel." That's a good hypothe-
sis. In fact, I believe that is what actually happened. Century
after century, the Church has drifted slightly from where it
was the century before. But that's hardly a reason to
discredit the Christians of the second century. Rather, it's a
good reason to discredit Christians of the *twentieth* century.
The second century Christians had less than one century of
drift; we have had nineteen.

Why I Believe the Gospel Remained Intact

How many denominations or religions do you know that
lost all of their basic doctrines and ordinances within a
century after their founders died? I don't know of any. The
conservative Reformed churches still teach today virtually all
of the same doctrines found in Calvin's *Institutes*. The
conservative Lutherans still hold to virtually all of the same
doctrines found in the Augsburg Confession. The conservative Anabaptists of today still hold to the same key
doctrines and practices of their sixteenth century ancestors.
The same is true of conservative Baptists and other groups.

Yet, we are nearly five hundred years removed from the
beginnings of those movements. Sure, there have been some
changes in all of these denominational groups. But the
changes have not been in key doctrinal areas or in the
primary Christian ordinances, such as baptism and communion. Views on peripheral issues, such as the gifts of the
Spirit, have changed in some of these groups. But not their
basic beliefs on salvation. Or the Trinity. Or the Incarnation.
Or man's fallen condition. They still baptize and have
communion the same way. *Spirituality* often wanes after one
generation, but not the cardinal doctrines and ordinances.

When we leave out theological liberals, Baptists today still
have the same basic beliefs and ordinances that Baptists did

in the last century. So do the Lutherans, the Methodists, the Mennonites, the Brethren, the Amish, the Nazarenes, the Salvation Army, the Church of Christ, and most other denominations.

And here we are talking about mere *man-made* denominations. Is our workmanship better than that of Christ and his apostles? (1 Cor. 3:11-15). Our workmanship has withstood the test of time. Do we really believe that theirs didn't? Did they build out of wood, hay, and stubble that didn't even last one century? Even man-made religions, such as Islam and Buddhism, have done better than that!

Besides, throughout the history of the Church, every major change in doctrines, ordinances, or moral teachings has always been accompanied with some sort of controversy. Invariably, someone in the group doesn't go along with the change. And we have a record of the controversy. The work of every one of the sixteenth-century Reformers was surrounded by conflict with the existing Church and with the other Reformers. Are we to believe that the cardinal teachings and ordinances of Christianity changed within a few decades after the end of the first century—all without any conflicts, debates, or dissenting congregations?

It would be the equivalent of the entire Roman Catholic Church having changed from its traditional beliefs to those of the Anabaptists—all within a few decades, and all without any controversy, dissenters, or discussion. And without even any record of *who* introduced such changes.

Today, we live in a fast-changing society; a society where change is *expected*. Change is usually welcomed today. But this trend is a new phenomenon in human history. In fact, our society has changed more in the past 250 years than it did in the previous *four thousand* years. Before the Industrial Revolution and the political revolutions of the 1700s, people strongly believed in doing things the way their ancestors did them. This was true in both the secular and the religious realms.

We are so used to change today, that we find it hard to believe that any society or church could exist for a century without change. Yet, the beliefs and practices of the traditional Eastern and Oriental Orthodox churches are virtually unchanged from the eighth century! Actually, they have had very little *theological* change since the end of the fourth century.

Even today, most of the major doctrinal changes that arise within a church or denomination are generally a result of the modernist or liberal movements of the past few centuries. By "liberal" or "modernist," I'm referring to the movements that question the inspiration or doctrinal inerrancy of Scripture. Yet, those movements are a fairly new phenomenon. There was no such movement in ancient times—certainly not in the second century Church.

Moreover, in *any* time period, churches under secular persecution are usually not innovators of new doctrines. How much new theology in this century has come out of eastern Europe or other places where the Church has been oppressed? Through the ages, virtually all of the doctrinal changes and theological controversies have taken place in that portion of the Church that was free from secular persecution. In fact, when Constantine and Licinius gave legal recognition to Christianity in A.D. 313, it sparked theological squabbles that lasted for centuries.

I am not saying that there was *no* change between the first and second centuries. I'm saying that the changes were small and that they were not in the areas of the major doctrines, ordinances, or moral teachings. This is substantiated by comparing the Church of the second century with that of the third. There was a small measure of drift between those centuries, but not in the primary doctrines, ordinances, or moral teachings. There were a few minor theological changes or, at least, changes in emphasis. There were some changes in theological terminology and in ecclesiastical structure. And there appears to have been more spiritual laxity in the third century. But, overall, there is relatively little difference between the two centuries.

But Didn't the Apostles Predict a Major Falling Away?

"Yes, but the apostles predicted there would be a major apostasy right after they passed away," several people have pointed out to me. And, it is true that the apostles did predict that false teachers would arise in their absence. But let's take a closer look at what the apostles actually did say would happen.

Paul told the Ephesian elders, "Be on guard for yourselves and for all the flock, among which the Holy Spirit has made you overseers, to shepherd the church of God which He purchased with His own blood. I know that after my departure savage wolves will come in among you, not sparing the flock; and from among your own selves men will arise, speaking perverse things, to draw away the disciples after them. Therefore be on the alert" (Acts 20:28-31).

And all of these things happened, just as Paul predicted. Teachers did arise towards the end of the apostolic age, saying perverse things and drawing away disciples after themselves. But we don't have to guess who those people were. We know their names. Names such as Cerinthus, Basilides, Valentinus, and Marcion.

And we know exactly what they taught, because a sizable portion of the early Christian works are directed against these false teachers. Most of those men to whom Paul was referring taught a form of heresy known as gnosticism. The gnostics claimed to have special supernatural knowledge (Gr. *gnosis)* that the rest of the church did not have. Gnostic teachings fit precisely what the apostles predicted.

For example, Paul wrote to Timothy, "But the Spirit explicitly says that in later times some will fall away from the faith, paying attention to deceitful spirits and doctrines of demons, . . . *men* who forbid marriage *and advocate* abstaining from foods, which God has created to be gratefully shared in by those who believe and know the truth" (1 Tim. 4:1,3). That is exactly what some of the gnostic groups taught. They had obligatory fasts and diets. Some of them even forbade marriage altogether. At the end of his letter to Timothy, Paul apparently was referring to the *gnostics: "O Timothy, guard what has been entrusted to you, avoiding worldly *and* empty chatter *and* the opposing arguments of what is falsely called 'knowledge'" (1 Tim. 6:20).

The apostle John also gave a description of the deceivers that had come forth by the end of the first century: "For many deceivers have gone out into the world, those who do not acknowledge Jesus Christ *as* coming in the flesh. This is the deceiver and the antichrist" (2 John 7). The gnostics were precisely the ones who did "not acknowledge Jesus Christ as coming in the flesh." Most of them taught that Jesus did not have a real body of flesh and blood. For, according to their teaching, an inferior god created our human bodies.

So the deceivers and false teachers that the apostles wrote about were the various gnostic teachers who arose by the end

---

*Gnosticism didn't reach its fully developed systems until the close of the first century. However, the beginnings of gnostic thought were evidently around in Paul's day. Several of the early Christians point to Simon Magus (Acts 8:9-24) as one of the founders of gnosticism.

of the first century. And they did pull some away from the true faith. But the apostles never said that the *whole* Church would fall away. Jesus declared just the opposite, "Upon this rock I will build My church; and the gates of Hades shall not overpower it" (Matt. 16:18). No, the apostles built their work with gold, silver, and precious stones. It withstood both the fiery trial of persecution and the test of false teachers. The apostles had adequately forewarned the Church of what was to come, and the Church was ready for it.

21

Did the New Testament Church Collapse?

About a year ago, I received a letter from a man who claimed that not only was the second century Church apostate, but the *first century* Church was as well! As evidence of this, he pointed to the presence of the Judaizers and to the rebukes given the seven churches described in Revelation.

In referring to the Judaizers, he claimed that, by the middle of the first century, the churches had already lost the gospel and had to be corrected by Paul. But that's not true. The problem with the Judaizers was not that *they* had changed the gospel, but that *God* had changed the gospel.* After all, Jesus had said, "Do not think that I came to abolish the Law or the Prophets; I did not come to abolish,

---

*i.e., there was a change from man's perspective. God's eternal purpose, of course, has never changed.

153

but to fulfill" (Matt. 5:17). The Law was given to mankind by God; it was not a human work. When the Church was initially founded, persons had to become Jews and live by the Law in order to become Christians. Male converts had to be circumcised.

But then God changed the rules. He broke down the wall of separation between the Jews and the Gentiles. Yet, it took a miraculous vision and a direct voice from the Holy Spirit to first bring this change about (Acts 10:9-22). The problem with the Judaizers was not that they were innovators of a new, corrupt gospel. It's just the opposite. They refused to change even when God instituted a change. They had not lost the *original* gospel. Instead, they clung to the original gospel and refused to accept God's modifications to it.

And although it took a lot of work on the part of the apostles, they did eventually silence the Judaizers. By the beginning of the second century, the Church was predominately Gentile. The Judaizers had either left the Church or had become a silent minority. They were no longer an issue by the second century.

The Seven Churches of Revelation

"But what about the seven churches of Revelation? Weren't they theologically apostate?" some have asked. It's certainly true that the letters or messages Jesus sent to those churches reveal that most of them had spiritual problems. However, their problems were not *theological*. Rather, their problems were moral. It was their *works* that were at fault (Rev. 2:5, 3:1,2,15). There has been some confusion about this because in the language of the King James Version, Jesus rebuked several churches for holding to the "doctrines" of the Nicolaitans, Balaam, or Jezebel. In the days of King James, the word "doctrines" commonly meant "teachings."

Today, we normally reserve the word "doctrines" to refer to *theological* teachings. But in the days of King James, the word was used in a broader sense.

The teachings of the Nicolaitans, Balaam, and Jezebel were not theological teachings. They were teachings of immorality and/or idolatry. As to the teachings of Balaam and Jezebel, Revelation itself makes this clear: "You have there some who hold the teaching of Balaam, who kept teaching Balak to put a stumbling block before the sons of Israel, to eat things sacrificed to idols, and to commit *acts of immorality*. . . . You tolerate the woman Jezebel, who calls herself a prophetess, and she teaches and leads My bond-servants astray, so that they commit *acts of* immorality and eat things sacrificed to idols" (Rev. 2:14,20).

A couple of the second century writers describe the Nicolaitans for us.[1] They reveal that this sect taught and practiced wife-swapping and other immoralities. Their erroneous "doctrines" or teachings did not involve theology.

So Scripture does not indicate that the church had become theologically corrupt by the time Revelation was written. In fact, it discloses just the opposite. It indicates that at the close of the first century, Jesus had no corrections to make to the theology and ordinances of the churches.* Jesus told the church in Thyatira, "But I say to you, the rest who are in Thyatira, who do not hold this teaching [of Jezebel], who have not known the deep things of Satan, as they call them—I place no other burden on you. Nevertheless what you have, hold fast until I come" (Rev. 2:24). He didn't tell

---

*Their primary problem was that they were lax in their church discipline. Immoral and/or idolatrous people like the Nicolaitans and the woman Jezebel needed to be put out of the Church. The record of the second century Church indicates that the churches took Jesus' words to heart and corrected this laxity in discipline.

them to *correct* what they had. No, He told them to hold fast to it until He returns. He told the church in Philadelphia the same thing (Rev. 3:11). Have *we* held fast to those same beliefs and practices?

Furthermore, Jesus had no correction whatsoever for two of the churches: Smyrna and Philadelphia. He described the church at Smyrna as being spiritually rich. That is significant because one of the personal disciples of the Apostle John at Smyrna was a man named Polycarp. He was almost certainly part of the church at Smyrna when Revelation was written, and he very likely was an elder there at the time.

Polycarp lived until the year A.D. 155 or later. He was at least 86 years old when he died as a faithful martyr. The churches to whom the second century orthodox writers belonged were all churches that were in communion with the church at Smyrna. In his letter to the Philippians, Polycarp specifically mentioned one of those writers, Ignatius, saying:

> I am sending you Ignatius's letters, as you request-
> ed; the ones he wrote to us, and some others that we
> had in our possession. They are enclosed herewith;
> you will be able to derive a great deal of benefit from
> them, for they tell you all about faith, and persever-
> ance, and all the ways of self-improvement that
> involve our Lord.[2]

As I have mentioned, another second century bishop and writer, Irenaeus, was a personal student of Polycarp. He testified that the church of his day (c.180) was still holding to the same gospel as that known by Polycarp.[3] He was in communication with the church in Smyrna, and he had personally visited the church in Rome. He quoted approving-ly from one of the works of Justin Martyr, evidencing the fact that Justin's gospel was no different than that of Irenaeus in France, or than that of the church in Smyrna.

In short, neither history, nor common sense, nor Scripture supports the conjecture that the entire Church went apostate shortly after the apostles died.

Were There Other Groups?

"But maybe the *entire* Church did not become apostate," some have conjectured. "Maybe there were some other groups in the second century about whom we don't know, but who believed like we do today."

What would make a person speculate about something for which there is no evidence? It's because they instinctively realize that apostolic Christianity could not have simply vanished into thin air within a few decades after the apostles died. They realize they must find a historic link. Yet, their mind is closed to the possibility that apostolic Christianity might have been different from *their* Christianity.

There is essentially no room to speculate about the existence of some second century splinter group that held to beliefs just like all of those commonly taught today. That's because about a third of the early Christian works pertain to the heresies of their day. One of them is even entitled, *The Refutation of All Heresies*. So we know the teachings of the groups that were not part of the main body of believers.

In addition, in those days Christians neither persecuted heretics nor ordered their books to be burned. Therefore, a fairly large amount of heretical writings from the second and third century have survived to our day. The most famous example is the collection of gnostic writings found near the Egyptian town of Nag Hammadi in 1945. So we know what the early heretics taught from their own writings. And I'm quite certain that few Christians today would want to claim any of those groups as their ancestors.

In summary, there simply is no historic primitive Church other than the one we have been talking about. So where does this leave us? It leaves us with a hard choice that few of us want to face.

22

The Hard Choice

The choices we have left are not easy. On the one hand, we can ignore the historic evidence. If we do that, we will continue to tear apart the body of Christ, breaking Christ's heart further.

On the other hand, we can swallow our sectarian pride. We can admit that as a church, we evangelical Protestants have failed miserably. We have trumpeted the motto, "Sola Scriptura," yet we haven't even been true to our own motto. Instead of getting back to "just the Bible," we have added our own sectarian traditions to Scripture.

The churches born out of the Reformation have been like the proverbial Humpty Dumpty who couldn't be put back together again. We Protestants have *never* been able to exist together as one united body. In fact, just a few hundred years ago, we were imprisoning, torturing, and hanging other Protestants, such as the Anabaptists, Brethren, Quakers, and dissenting evangelicals.

In our great learning and wisdom, we turn our noses up at the teachings and practices of the early Church. But perhaps we would do well to listen to what Irenaeus told the gnostic sects of his day. After all, his description of the gnostic sects sounds curiously similar to our Protestant sects:

> As many of them as there are, they depart from each other, holding so many different opinions as to one thing, and bearing about their clever notions in secret within themselves. When, therefore, they have all agreed among themselves as to the things written beforehand in the Scriptures, then they still will be refuted by us. In the meanwhile, in addition to holding wrong beliefs, they condemn themselves anyway. For they are not of one mind with regard to the same things. In contrast, we follow the one and only true God as our teacher. We possess His words as the rule of truth. And we do all speak alike with regard to the same things.[1]

We are so quick to correct the early Christians for their theological "errors," yet it is we who need to learn from them. When *we* have shown that we can all be one, maybe then we can instruct them. Until then, what we need is some heartfelt repentance for our sectarian spirit. If the Corinthian church couldn't properly come together for communion because of their conflicts, are our communions acceptable to God? (1 Cor. 11:17-20). Paul rebuked the Corinthians for their divisions, saying: "You are still carnal. For where there are envy, strife, and *divisions* among you, are you not carnal and behaving like mere men?" (1 Cor. 3:3 NKJV italics mine). Maybe that's what we are—carnal men and women in need of a godly rebuke.

My Decision

I will tell you what decision I have made. As I have mentioned, at first I fought bitterly against the things I was finding in the historic record of the Church. But eventually I yielded when I realized how thoroughly Biblical their Christianity was. I knew that I had to be at one with them. I shared these things with my family, and we prayed about it. And as a family we made a commitment to turn our lives around.

It was the only decision to make. As a lawyer, I knew how I would approach the writings of the apostles if they had been contracts or deeds. Without hesitation, I would have looked at the "course of performance" as evidenced by the second century writings. It was the common sense thing to do.

When my eternal life and my relationship with God were at stake, could I be any less exacting? Didn't I still have to look at the "course of performance"? And once I read the Scriptures through the eyes of the primitive Church, I knew I never wanted to read them again through the tint of my twentieth century glasses.

I realized that one of two things had happened or was going to happen: Either the primitive Christians had had a rude awakening after they had died and found out how apostate *they* had been. Or I was going to have a rude awakening after I died and found out how apostate *I* had been. The latter seemed to be the more likely event. So I decided I would rather have the rude awakening *now*. So did my family.

That is not to say that our lifestyle and our views have changed overnight. It has taken us several years to flush out some of our old ways of thinking. And we still have a long way to go. But we have committed ourselves to make these changes together as a family. Some people have criticized us for moving too slowly; others think we're extremists. However, the only opinion we care about is God's.

What Will Your Decision Be?

But now the ball is in your court. What will you do? The easiest course of action will be to ignore this book and to forget that the early Christians even existed. It will be far easier to retreat back to the comfort of your denomination, safely protected by its seminaries and theological literature.

Or perhaps you will satisfy yourself by finding loopholes or imperfections in this common sense approach to understanding Scripture. Admittedly, it is not a perfect system. Winston Churchill once said, "Democracy is the worst form of Government—except all those other forms that have been tried."[2] The same thing could be said about my common sense approach. It's the worst system there is—except for all the rest.

The *best* system would be to ask the Bible writers themselves what they meant. But that option is closed. The second best system would be to ask the New Testament congregations what the apostles meant. But that option is closed, too. The third best system would be to ask the next generation of Christians. That option is available. It's a third-best system, but it's the best we have.

I realize that I have addressed some matters in this book that many of my readers will find disturbing. These very same things unsettled me originally. However, I have shared these painful things with you only because I want something very wonderful for you—and for the entire Church.

If You Have Decided To Ignore This Book

If you have already decided to reject this approach to Scripture, I want to ask you: What is *your* solution? What system of interpretation do *you* propose that can bring together in one body all of us who love God and believe the Bible?

Please don't say, "Well, if everyone would just go by the Bible, we could all be one." We've already hashed that out. That was Plan A. That's what the Reformers tried. That's what millions of Christians have been trying ever since. Plan A hasn't worked, because we can't agree on what the Bible teaches.

If Plan A had worked, I wouldn't have bothered to write this book. But since it didn't work, we need to try Plan B—the "common sense" approach. But if you're not willing to try Plan B, let me ask you again: what is *your* plan?

After all, if you and I aren't working for a solution to the divisions in the body of Christ, we are part of the problem. We can't plead innocence to Jesus and say, "It wasn't our fault Your Body was so divided. There was nothing we could do about it." There *is* something we can do about it. We can try Plan B. Or if someone has a better plan, he or she can let us all know about it so that we can try that plan.

We All Once Had Open Minds

At one time, every one of us had a mind that was open to hear God's truth. This may have been when we were children. Or it may have been when we were converted from godless lives to Christianity. Or perhaps it was when we grew disillusioned with the group in which we were raised.

Whenever it was, our minds were once truly open to hear what God had to say.

But when our minds were open, did anyone bother to explain to us what the early Christians believed? Were their beliefs and practices ever set before us as an alternate course to follow? I know that nobody ever gave *me* that opportunity. Nor is it likely that it was ever given to you.

So our entire belief systems were formed without our ever having been given the opportunity to try out historic Christianity. Unfortunately, now our belief systems are already established, so it's difficult for us to objectively look at early Christianity. Yet, we owe it to ourselves to take at least one honest, objective look. We deserve to see what Christianity was like in its primitive years.

Of White Rats And Men

In college, our science professor once told us about an experiment with white rats. The purpose of the experiment, he told us, was to provide additional evidence that children who are abused or emotionally starved do not learn as quickly as more privileged children. The researchers wanted to demonstrate that principle using two groups of white rats.

The researchers hand fed the rats in Group A. They gently petted them several times a day, and even spoke softly to them. In contrast, they had no personal contact with the rats in Group B. Those rats had been dumped into a cage and were fed through a sliding door. After about a month of this treatment, it was time to see how quickly the two groups of rats would learn their way through a maze.

So the researchers called in a group of college science students. They introduced the students to the two groups of rats and explained to them the differences in treatment. They demonstrated the series of tests the students were to run on the rats. The students were then left alone to conduct the experiments. To no one's surprise, the students found that the rats in Group A learned more quickly than the "underprivileged" rats in Group B.

But then came the real surprise: the entire experiment was a hoax. There never had been *two* groups of rats. Rather, until the day of the maze tests, all of the rats had been together. All of them had been treated alike. They had been divided into Groups A and B only moments before the students had arrived.

Why then did the experiments show Group A to learn faster? Because the students already had a preconceived notion that those rats would learn faster. They let their preconceptions affect their observations of the rats. The real experiment had been to demonstrate the effect of preconceived notions. And it had demonstrated it well.

Like those students, you will only be wasting your time if you read the early Christian writings through the tinted glasses of your preconceived theological views. Your biases will color everything you read. So before reading, it is essential that you *temporarily* set aside all of your beliefs. Then simply listen to what the historical record has to say. Let your mind be transported back to the first and second centuries. Breathe in the culture and thought patterns of that age.

As you read, remember that these writings are not some kind of "second canon." The personal views and idiosyncrasies of each writer are not particularly important. Your quest is to find out how the primitive Church in general understood the New Testament. In other words, what was the "course of performance" of the first generations of Christians?

After you have read enough of their works to have a good feel for their culture, mindset, and overall Christian beliefs, go back and re-read the New Testament. Read it through *their* pattern of thinking. See what new things you will discover. When you're all through, you're free to go back and pick up all of your former beliefs, if you like.

But perhaps you never will.

Appendix

Sources of Early Christian Writings

• *The Ante-Nicene Fathers*, published by Wm. B. Eerdmans Publishing Company, 255 Jefferson Ave. S. E., Grand Rapids, MI 49503. $299.00. This ten volume set contains nearly all of the writings of the pre-Nicene Church (with the exception of much of Origen's writings), save for a few works discovered in the twentieth century. This set is the most economical way to obtain the vast bulk of the early Christian writings. The set can be obtained through Scroll Publishing Co., and through some mail order distributors, at nearly half price. The translations in this series are fairly literal, making them ideal for serious, unbiased study of what the early Christians believed. However, the literalness of the translations, coupled with the translators' use of archaic and academic language, means that these are not the easiest of translations to read.

• *Early Christian Writings*, translated by Maxwell Staniforth, published by Viking Penguin Inc., 40 West 23rd St., New York, New York 10010. $5.95. This paperback book contains some of the earliest writings of the primitive Church: the Didache, the letter to Diognetus, Martyrdom of Polycarp, and the letters of Clement of Rome, Ignatius,

Polycarp, and Barnabas. This translation into contemporary English is quite readable, although it is not as literal as *The Ante-Nicene Fathers*.

• *Early Christian Fathers*, translated by Cyril C. Richardson, published by Macmillan Publishing Co., Inc., New York. $11.95. This paperback translation contains the Didache, Martyrdom of Polycarp, Second Clement, the letter to Diognetus, the First Apology of Justin Martyr, the apology of Athenagoras, selections from the works of Irenaeus, and the letters of Clement of Rome, Ignatius, and Polycarp.

• *The Apostolic Fathers* (2nd Edition), translated by J. B. Lightfoot, published by Baker Book House, Grand Rapids, Michigan 49616. $17.95. This translation, which has been revised into contemporary English, contains the Didache, the Martyrdom of Polycarp, Second Clement, the letter to Diognetus, the Shepherd of Hermas, fragments of Papias, and the letters of Clement of Rome, Ignatius, Barnabas, and Polycarp.

• **Scroll Publishing Co.**, P. O. Box 6175, Tyler, Texas 75711 publishes The Didache in booklet form ($ .95), along with easy-to-read renditions of some of the works of Justin Martyr, Mark Felix, Clement of Alexandria, and Tertullian. It also publishes a devotional work, *The Pilgrim Road*, taken entirely from early Christian writings. ($7.95).

• **Paulist Press**, 997 Macarthur Blvd., Mahwah, N. J. 07430 publishes the Ancient Christian Writers series, which contains contemporary translations of many of the pre-Nicene Christian writers (over 18 volumes), along with numerous post-Nicene writers. For the equivalent amount of material, these hardbound volumes are considerably more expensive than *The Ante-Nicene Fathers,* but the translations are easier to read. Two of the volumes contain works that are not included in *The Ante-Nicene Fathers:* Irenaeus' "Proof of the Apostolic Preaching" and Origen's commentary and sermons on the Song of Solomon. Prices per volume range from $14.95 to $24.95.

Paulist Press also publishes a paperback edition of some of Origen's writings, several of which are not included in *The Ante-Nicene Fathers,* such as "An Exhortation to Martyrdom" and "On Prayer." $9.95.

• **The Catholic University of America Press,** P. O. Box 4852, Hampden Station, Baltimore, MD 21211, publishes The Fathers of the Church series that contains several volumes of pre-Nicene writings, translated into contemporary English. One of the volumes contains Origen's *Homilies on Genesis and Exodus,* which are not included in *The Ante-Nicene Fathers.* Average price per volume is $14.95.

Most of the works described above can be purchased through your local Christian bookstore. If not, they can be purchased directly from the various publishers or through Scroll Publishing Co. For a free catalog of early Christian writings and other source material, write to Scroll Publishing, P. O. Box 6175, Tyler, Texas 75711.

Note: All prices quoted above are the approximate prices as of January, 1992. Before ordering any of the works listed, please ascertain the current price.

Notes

Chapter One: The Mad Philosopher

1. Jeffery L. Sheler, "Reuniting the flock," *U. S. News & World Report,* March 4, 1991, p. 50.

Chapter Two: A Tale of Two Lawyers

1. Samuel Butler, *The Way of All Flesh* (New York: Holt, Rinehart and Winston, 1963), p. 106.

2. Martin Luther, *The Bondage of the Will,* trans. Henry Cole (Grand Rapids: Baker Book House, 1976), p. 14.

Chapter Three: Rules of Truth

1. Winston Churchill, quoted in Frank S. Mead, *12,000 Religious Quotations* (Grand Rapids: Baker Book House, 1989), p. 450.

Chapter Four: Principles of Interpretation

1. Martin Luther, *Works of Martin Luther*, ed. Henry Eyster Jacobs, vol. 6 (Grand Rapids: Baker Book House, 1982), p. 447.

2. *Restatement of the Law, Contracts (2d),* (St. Paul: American Law Institute Publishers, 1973), p. 510.

3. Ibid.

Chapter Five: Why Human Language Is Unclear

1. Martin Luther, *The Bondage of the Will,* trans. Henry Cole (Grand Rapids: Baker Book House, 1976), pp. 27, 29, 108, 109.

Chapter Nine: The Horse's Mouth

1. Justin *First Apology* 14.

2. Unknown author *Letter to Diognetus* 1.

3. Clement *Miscellanies* 1.1.

4. Irenaeus *Against Heresies* 1.10.1,2, trans. Cyril C. Richardson (New York: Macmillan Publishing Co., Inc., 1970), pp. 360, 361.

5. Ibid. 3.3.4, pp. 373, 374.

6. Irenaeus *Against Heresies* 3.1-4; Clement *Miscellanies* 7.16; Tertullian *Against Heretics* 6, 21, 22.

Chapter Ten: The Answer

1. Lit., "who have fallen into wedlock," a reflection of Tertullian's Montanism, reflecting a low view of marriage.

2. Tertullian, *A Glimpse At Early Christian Church Life*, trans. David W. Bercot: "The Veiling of Virgins" (Tyler, TX: Scroll Publishing Co., 1991), pp. 150, 151.

3. Ibid., pp. 125, 138.

4. Clement *The Instructor* 3.12.

5. Hippolytus *Apostolic Tradition* 18.

6. Some examples of pictures from the early Church are contained in the booklet, *Let Her Be Veiled*, Tom Shank, ed. (Kalispell, MT: Torch Publications, 1988), pp. 42-49.

7. *Restatement of the Law, Contracts (2d)*, (St. Paul: American Law Institute Publishers, 1973), p. 516.

Chapter Twelve: The Forgotten Septuagint

1. George Howard, "The Septuagint: A Review of Recent Studies," an essay contained in: Sidney Jellicoe, ed., *Studies In The Septuagint: Origins, Recensions, and Interpretations* (New York: KTAV Publishing House, Inc., 1974), pp. 60, 61.

2. *The International Standard Bible Encyclopedia*, s. v. "Septuagint," by S. K. Soderlund.

3. Dikran Y. Hadidian, "The Septuagint and its Place in Theological Education," *The Expository Times*, Vol. 76, 1964.

Chapter Thirteen: Other Bombshells

1. Edgar J. Goodspeed, Preface to *The Apocrypha* (New York: Random House, Inc., 1959), pp. vii, viii.

2. Josh McDowell, *Evidence That Demands A Verdict* (San Bernadino, CA: Here's Life Publishers, Inc., 1979), p. 33.

3. For example, see Justin Martyr *Dialogue with Trypho, a Jew*.

Chapter Fourteen: What We Would Rather Not See

1. Rudyard Kipling, "The Ballad of East and West," quoted in *The Oxford Dictionary of Quotations* (London: Oxford University Press, 1955), p. 294.

2. Barnabas *Epistle* 10, trans. Maxwell Staniforth, *Early Christian Writings* (New York: Viking Penguin Inc., 1987), p. 170.

3. David W. Bercot, *Will The Real Heretics Please Stand Up* (Tyler, TX: Scroll Publishing Co., 1989), pp. 42,43.

Chapter Fifteen: The Real Issue

1. J. Harold Greenlee, quoted in Josh McDowell, *Evidence That Demands A Verdict* (San Bernadino, CA: Here's Life Publishers, Inc., 1979), p. 50.

2. Fritz Ridenour, *So What's the Difference?* (Glendale, CA: G/L Publications, 1967), p. iii.

3. Josh McDowell and Don Stewart, *Handbook of Today's Religions* (San Bernadino, CA: Here's Life Publishers, Inc., 1983), p. 17.

Chapter Sixteen: The Myth of "Sola Scriptura"

1. Martin Luther, *Works of Martin Luther*, ed. Henry Eyster Jacobs, vol. 6 (Grand Rapids: Baker Book House, 1982), pp. 439-444.

2. William Tyndale, modern spelling by David Daniell, *Tyndale's New Testament* (New Haven, CT: Yale University Press, 1989).

3. Ibid.

4. *Geneva Bible: A Facsimile of the 1560 Edition* (Madison, WI: University of Wisconsin Press, 1969).

5. Ibid.

Chapter Seventeen: The Catch

1. *Webster's New World Dictionary of the American Language* (New York: The World Publishing Company, 1960), p. 1544.

2. Irenaeus *Fragments* 3; Hippolytus *Refutation* 8.6.

Chapter Eighteen: The Other Catch

1. Martin Luther, quoted in Philip Schaff, *History of the Christian Church*, vol. VII: *Modern Christianity* (Grand Rapids: Eerdmans Publishing Company, 1910), p. 362.

2. *Bookstore Journal*, January 1992, p. 194.

3. From the preface to the first edition of *Living Letters* (Wheaton, IL: Tyndale House Publishers, 1962).

4. *Bookstore Journal*, January 1992, p. 194.

5. The significance of this alteration of Scripture pertains to the role of fleshly Israel in the fulfillment of Bible prophecies.

6. Galatians 5:13-26 is a similar passage where Paul again talks about the flesh being in opposition to the Spirit, or the spirit. He describes the fruits of the flesh and the fruits of the Spirit or spirit. I had always understood the fruits of the Spirit to be talking about the fruits of the Holy Spirit. Yet, Paul could have been talking about the fruits of our human spirit, what he calls the "inner man" at Romans 7:22.

Chapter Nineteen: Sincere Questions About the Early Church Writings

1. Jeffery L. Sheler, "Reuniting the flock," *U. S. News & World Report*, March 4, 1991, p. 50.

2. For example, contrast the orthodox work of Tertullian, *The Prescription Against Heretics* 22, with his Montanistic work, *On the Veiling of Virgins* 1. See also Irenaeus *Against Heresies* 3.1.1-3.4.3.

3. Irenaeus *Against Heresies* 3.2.2.

4. Johannes Quasten, *Patrology,* vol. 1 (Westminster, MD: Christian Classics, Inc., 1988), p. 10.

5. Some examples of books that claim that Paul and/or the other apostles derived their teachings from Greek thought are: *Jesus and the Greeks*, by

William Fairweather; *Jew and Greek*, by MacGregor and Purdy; *Greek Thought in the New Testament*, by George Holley Gilbert; and *The Ancient World* by Thomas W. Africa. Some of the books that claim that some Christian teachings were derived from the Qumran community are: *Judaism and the Origins of Christianity* by David Flusser and *Paul and Qumran* by Jerome Murphy-O' Connor.

6. Tertullian *A Treatise on the Soul* 3. Tertullian was adamant in his opposition to the Greek philosophers. See, for example, his *Apology* 46,47.

7. Nobody seems to know who authored this slogan. It has been credited to various Christians, including Philip Melanchthon, Peter Meiderlin, and Richard Baxter.

Chapter Twenty: Did the Church Remain Faithful?
1. Irenaeus *Against Heresies* 3.1-4; Clement *Miscellanies* 7.16; Tertullian *Against Heretics* 6, 21, 22.

Chapter Twenty-One: Did the New Testament Church Collapse?
1. Irenaeus *Against Heresies* 1.26.3; Clement *Miscellanies* 3.4.

2. Polycarp *Letter to the Philippians* 13, trans. Maxwell Staniforth, *Early Christian Writings* (New York: Viking Penguin Inc., 1987), p. 124.

3. Irenaeus *Against Heresies* 3.3.

Chapter Twenty-Two: The Hard Choice
1. Irenaeus *Against Heresies* 4.35.4.

2. Winston Churchill, *Winston S. Churchill: His Complete Speeches, 1897-1963*, ed. Robert Rhodes James, vol. 7 (1974), p. 7566.

For a free catalog of early Christian writings, Jewish spiritual works (such as the Book of Enoch), and books about early Christianity and radical Christian living today, write:

Scroll Publishing Co.
P. O. Box 6175
Tyler, TX 75711
(903) 597-8023